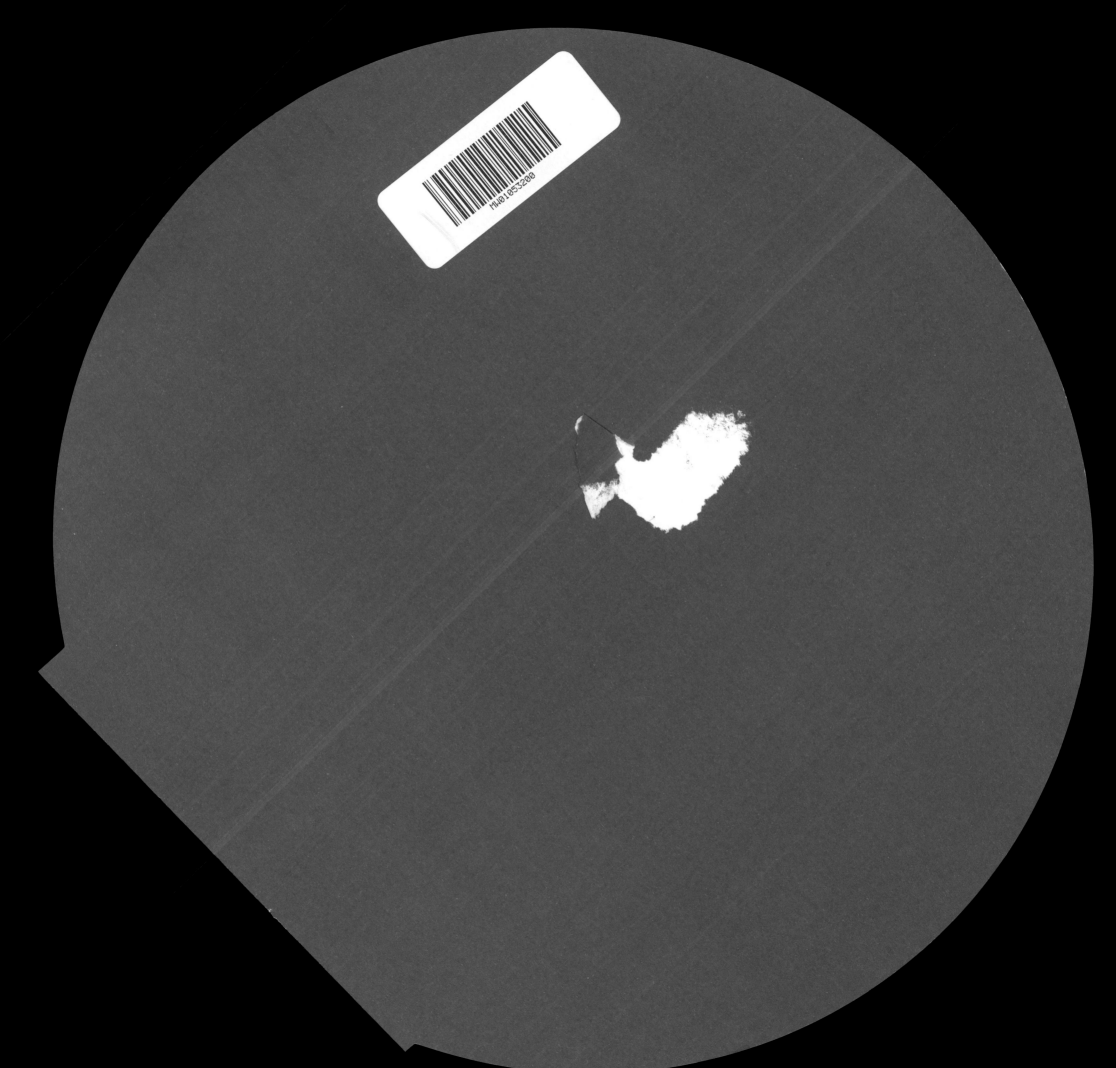

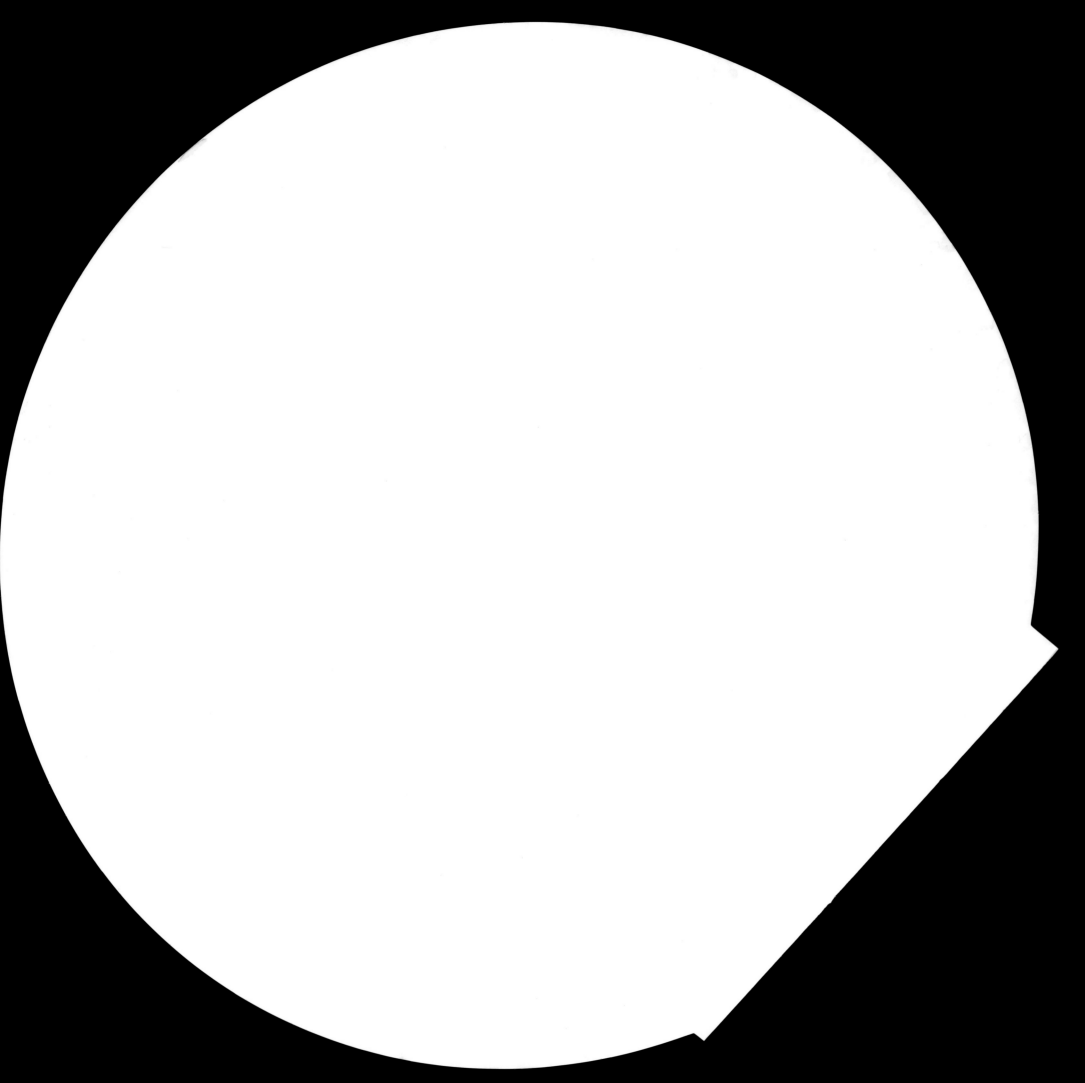

Pies
Tarts

How to Make More Than
50 Scrumptious Pies and Tarts

Carla Bardi • Rachel Lane

Reader's Digest

The Reader's Digest Association, Inc.
New York, NY

FOR McRAE PUBLISHING
Project Director Anne McRae
Art Director Marco Nardi
Photography Brent Parker Jones, Paul Nelson (R&R PhotoStudio)
Text Carla Bardi, Rachel Lane
Editing Foreign Concept
Food Styling Lee Blaylock, Rebecca Quinn
Layouts Aurora Granata
Prepress Filippo Delle Monache

FOR READER'S DIGEST
U.S. Project Editor Kim Casey
Cover Designer Jennifer Tokarski
Senior Art Director George McKeon
Executive Editor, Trade Publishing Dolores York
Associate Publisher, Trade Publishing Rosanne McManus
President and Publisher, Trade Publishing Harold Clarke

Library of Congress Cataloging-in-Publication Data

Lane, Rachel.
Pies and tarts : how to make over 60 scrumptious pies and tarts / Rachel Lane.
    p. cm.
"A Reader's Digest book."
ISBN 978-1-60652-250-9
1. Pies. 2. Cookbooks. I. Reader's Digest Association. II. Title.
TX773.L293 2011
641.8'652--dc22
                                    2010043087

NOTE TO OUR READERS
Eating eggs or egg whites that are not completely cooked poses the
possibility of salmonella food poisoning. The risk is greater for pregnant
women, the elderly, the very young, and persons with impaired immune
systems. If you are concerned about salmonella, you can use
reconstituted powdered egg whites or pasteurized eggs.

contents

tarts & pies

Cooks have been happily baking tarts and pies for eons. Archeologists working in Egypt have found traces of pielike dishes with rustic, free-form crusts topped with honey and baked over hot coals dating to over 11,500 years ago. The ancient Greeks and Romans also made pies, although they were filled with savory meats and wrapped in a flour-and-water crust. By the Middle Ages, many pies had sweet fillings, or a mixture of sweet and savory. A 13th-century recipe book from Andalusia in Spain, gave a detailed recipe for a pie stuffed with tortoises and baked in a crust of flour, eggs, and saffron. In Italy chefs liked to startle the guests at the banquets of their aristocratic bosses with huge pies that were stuffed full of live birds, which would fly out when the pie was cut. Some European pies were even large enough to hold dwarf minstrels, actors, or dancers who would burst from the pie and saunter down the banqueting table singing and dancing. But it was in England that pies were really taken to heart. Queen Elizabeth I was said to be especially fond of apple pie and cherry pie and is even rumored to have invented the latter. When the Pilgrims set sail for North America they took this English specialty with them and made it their own, giving rise to the saying "as American as apple pie," among others.

In this book you will find recipes for 57 mouthwatering pies, along with detailed instructions for preparing perfect crusts. The terms "tart" and "pie" are often used interchangeably, but we have tried to establish some order by calling most single-crust concoctions "tarts" and most double-crust creations "pies." We have also included a handful of delicious crumb-crust pies, made from crushed cookies and wafers. We hope you will enjoy baking and eating these pies as much as we have!

hints & tips

The secret to making the perfect tart or pie lies in the page 14. Take the time to follow the step-by-step crust. It should be both tender and crisp, as well as flaky, instructions and remember that making pastry is an art, but without being crumbly. It should have an excellent and the more often you make it, the more skilled you taste and be good enough to eat on its own without the will become.
topping or filling. In this book we have suggested two We have suggested that you use bleached all-purpose basic crusts—a rich, slightly sweet one (a *pâte sucrée*, as (plain) flour. Choose a good-quality brand and the the French call it) for tarts, and a light, buttery flaky results will be perfect. Do not use cake flour or bread one (a *pâte brisée*, in French) for pies. Instructions for flour. To make a whole-wheat (wholemeal) crust, preparing and prebaking these crusts are given on replace one-third of the all-purpose (plain) flour with pages 8–11 and are referred to throughout the book. whole-wheat flour. Be sure to use a high-quality, We have also included some special tarts and pies high-fat butter in all the crusts. The fat in the that have their own specific crusts. butter makes the crust tender and pie crusts
If you are a novice to tarts and pies, we proof. Remember that tart and pie crusts suggest that you begin with something were originally made with lard, which is 100 simple, such as the Strawberry Tart on percent fat. High-quality butter is about

Above: Cherry Tart (see recipe on page 54) goes beautifully with a spoonful of crème fraîche or whipped cream.

6

80 percent fat; lower-quality brands contain more water and will produce a less-than-tender crust.

We have offered two methods for mixing the dough: in a food processor and by hand. The food processor method is easier and quicker and will make an excellent crust, although it is very important not to overprocess the ingredients. For skilled bakers, the hand method will produce the lightest and flakiest crust. When the dough is mixed and you are kneading it briefly and shaping it into a disk for chilling, check to make sure that there are tiny flakes of butter visible beneath the surface of the dough; this means that it is not overmixed or overprocessed and will be flaky.

Tart and pie dough should be chilled to make it firmer and easier to roll without cracking. When it is rolled and in the pan, it can be chilled again before baking.

For tarts, we have suggested that you use a tart pan with a removable bottom, which makes it easier to slide the finished tart onto a serving plate without breaking. Most pies are served directly from the pan. When baking a double-crust pie, remember that the filling will produce steam that must escape; otherwise, the top of the pie will puff up in an unsightly way or the filling will burst the edges of the pie and seep out. To prevent this from happening, cut vents into the top of the pie with a sharp knife, so that the steam can escape.

Happy baking!

Above: Strawberry Tart (see recipe on page 14) is classic and simple. It makes a wonderful family dessert and an elegant offering with tea or coffee.

sweet tart crust pastry

1 ²/₃ cups (250 g) all-purpose (plain) flour
¹/₃ cup (65 g) superfine (caster) sugar · ¹/₄ teaspoon salt
²/₃ cup (150 g) unsalted butter, cold, cut in cubes · 1 large egg
2 tablespoons heavy (double) cream

FOR CHOCOLATE SWEET TART PASTRY: Use 1 ¹/₃ cups (200 g) all-purpose (plain) flour and ¹/₃ cup (50 g) unsweetened cocoa powder (instead of 1 ²/₃ cups [250 g] all-purpose [plain] flour)

SERVES 8 · PREPARATION 15 MINUTES · COOKING 10–15 MINUTES

FOOD PROCESSOR METHOD (BELOW)

1a. Combine the flour, sugar, and salt in a food processor with a metal blade. Pulse to combine. Add the butter and pulse briefly 12–15 times, until the mixture resembles coarse bread crumbs.

2a. Add the egg and cream, with the machine running. Pulse until the mixture just comes together.

BY HAND (BELOW)

1b. Stir the flour, sugar, and salt in a medium bowl or on a clean work surface. Use a pastry cutter to cut in the butter or rub it in with your hands until the mixture resembles coarse bread crumbs.

2b. Whisk the egg and cream in a small bowl. Stir into the butter-and-flour mixture with a wooden spoon.

3. (opposite page) Turn the dough out onto a sheet of plastic wrap (cling film). Press into a 6-inch (18-cm) disk and wrap in the plastic wrap. Chill in the refrigerator for at least 30 minutes (or up to 48 hours).

4. Lightly grease or spray an 11-inch

5. Unwrap the dough and place on a cool surface. A marble slab (available in gourmet food stores) is ideal, because it keeps the dough from softening too quickly. Flour the dough lightly on both sides.

(28-cm) tart pan with a removable bottom.

6. Roll the dough out between two sheets of plastic wrap (or parchment paper) until ⅛ inch (3 mm) thick and about 13 inches (33 cm) in diameter. Lift the plastic wrap away from the pastry from time to time, and dust with flour if it begins to stick. If the dough becomes too soft at any point, place in the refrigerator until it firms a little.

7. To transfer the dough to the pan, remove the top layer of plastic. Dust the rolling pin lightly with flour and loosely roll the pastry around it, removing the other layer of plastic as you work.

8. Gently lower the pastry on the rolling pin over the tart pan, unrolling it carefully and draping loosely over the pan. Using your fingers,

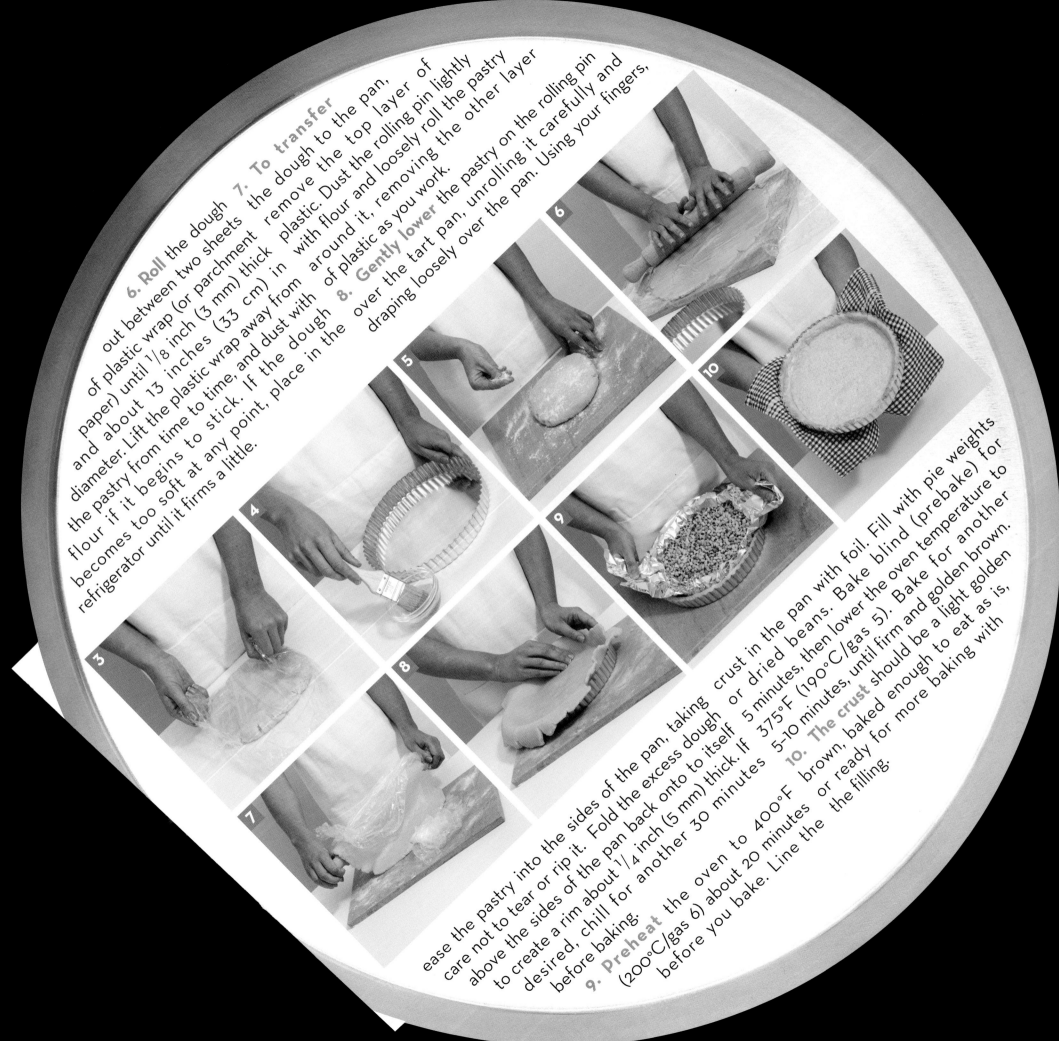

ease the pastry into the sides of the pan, taking care not to tear or rip it. Fold the excess dough above the sides of the pan back onto itself to create a rim about ¼ inch (5 mm) thick. If desired, chill for another 30 minutes before baking.

9. Preheat the oven to 400°F (200°C/gas 6) about 20 minutes before you bake. Line the crust in the pan with foil. Fill with pie weights or dried beans. Bake blind (prebake) for 5 minutes, then lower the oven temperature to 375°F (190°C/gas 5). Bake for another 5–10 minutes, until firm and golden brown.

10. The crust should be a light golden brown, baked enough to eat as is, or ready for more baking with the filling.

pie crust pastry

2²/₃ cups (400 g) all-purpose (plain) flour
¼ teaspoon salt • 1 cup (250 g) unsalted butter, cold, cut in cubes • 6–8 tablespoons (90–120 ml) iced water • 1 tablespoon cider vinegar

SERVES 8 • **PREPARATION** 15–20 MINUTES • **COOKING** 15–20 MINUTES

FOOD PROCESSOR METHOD (BELOW)

1a. Combine the flour and salt in a food processor with a metal blade. Pulse briefly to combine. Add the butter cubes and pulse until the mixture resembles coarse crumbs.

2a. Add 6 tablespoons (90 ml) of water and the cider vinegar and pulse 5–6 times. Pinch the mixture together in your fingers; if it does not hold together add another tablespoon of water. Pulse 2–3 times and test again. When ready the mixture will be in grains and will not hold together unless pinched.

BY HAND (BELOW)

1b. Combine the flour and salt in a medium bowl. Cut in the butter with a pastry cutter or rub it in with your fingertips until the mixture resembles coarse crumbs.

2b. Add 6 tablespoons (90 ml) of water and the cider vinegar and stir the mixture with a rubber spatula, squashing it against the sides of the bowl. Add enough of the remaining water to form a stiff dough.

3. Press the dough into a disk and wrap in plastic wrap (cling film). Chill in the refrigerator for 1 hour.

4. Unwrap the dough and divide in half (for a double-crust pie) or one piece slightly larger than the other (for a lattice-topped pie). Roll out one piece of dough (the larger piece if making a lattice-topped pie) on a cool work surface (preferably a marble slab) into a circle about 1/8 inch (3 mm) thick and about 12 inches (30 cm) in diameter. Work quickly so that the dough doesn't soften too much. Roll from the center where the dough is thicker to make an even layer. Wrap the remaining piece of dough and return to the refrigerator.

5. Roll the pastry loosely around the rolling pin and drape it carefully over the pie pan. Using your

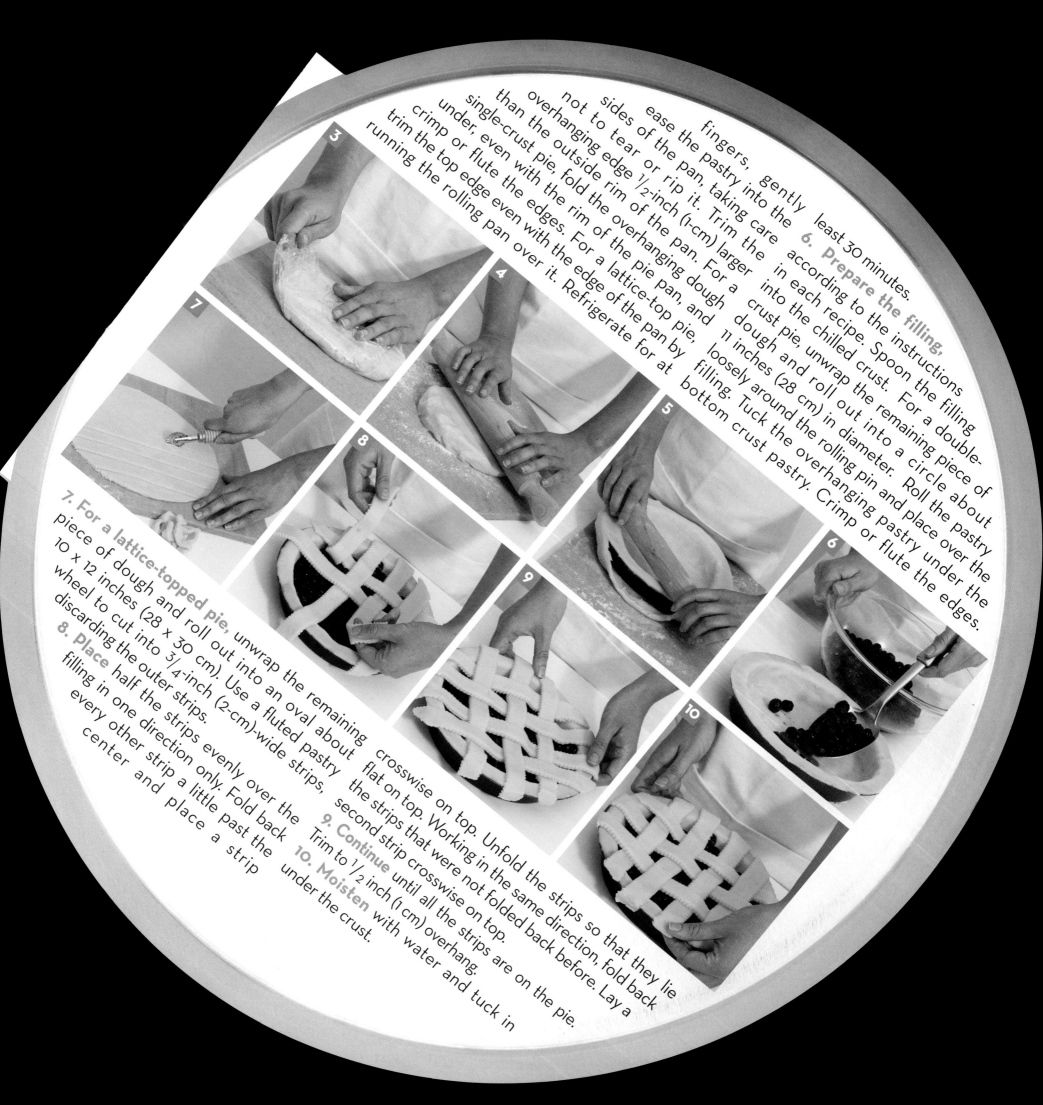

fingers, gently ease the pastry into the sides of the pan, taking care not to tear or rip it. Trim the overhanging edge ½-inch (1-cm) larger than the outside rim of the pan. For a single-crust pie, fold the overhanging dough under, even with the rim of the pie pan, and crimp or flute the edges. For a lattice-top pie, trim the top edge even with the edge of the pan by running the rolling pan over it. Refrigerate for at least 30 minutes.

6. Prepare the filling, according to the instructions in each recipe. Spoon the filling into the chilled crust. For a double-crust pie, unwrap the remaining dough and roll out into a circle about 11 inches (28 cm) in diameter. Roll the pastry loosely around the rolling pin and place over the filling. Tuck the overhanging pastry under the bottom crust pastry. Crimp or flute the edges.

7. For a lattice-topped pie, unwrap the remaining piece of dough and roll out into an oval about 10 x 12 inches (28 x 30 cm). Use a fluted pastry wheel to cut into 3/4-inch (2-cm)-wide strips, discarding the outer strips.

8. Place half the strips evenly over the filling in one direction only. Fold back every other strip a little past the center and place a strip crosswise on top. Unfold the strips so that they lie flat on top. Working in the same direction, fold back the strips that were not folded back before. Lay a second strip crosswise on top.

9. Continue until all the strips are on the pie. Trim to ½ inch (1 cm) overhang.

10. Moisten with water and tuck in under the crust.

CRUST

Sweet tart pastry (see pages 8–9)

LEMON FILLING

8 large eggs • 1½ cups (300 g) superfine (caster) sugar
1 cup (250 ml) freshly squeezed lemon juice • Finely grated zest of 3 lemons
1 cup (250 ml) heavy (double) cream

SERVES 8 • PREPARATION 45 MINUTES + 1 HOUR TO CHILL & COOL
COOKING 45–55 MINUTES

lemon tart

CRUST **1. Prepare** the sweet tart pastry and chill for at least 30 minutes. **2. Line** an 11-inch (28-cm) tart pan with a removable bottom with the pastry and bake blind following the instructions on page 9. FILLING **3. Preheat** the oven to 300°F (150°C/gas 2) and place a baking sheet in the oven. **4. Break** the eggs into a large bowl, add the superfine sugar, and whisk for a few seconds—the mixture shouldn't be frothy. **5. Strain** the lemon juice through a fine-mesh sieve. Pour the lemon juice, zest, and cream into the egg mixture and whisk until smooth. **6. Pour** the filling into the baked pastry crust. **7. Bake** for 35–40 minutes, until the filling is just set but still trembles a little in the center. **8. Let cool** to room temperature before serving.

This is a classic tart that can be made for any occasion all year round. Serve with fresh fruit or a spoonful of whipped cream.

● If you liked this recipe, try the orange ricotta tart on page 24.

strawberry tart

CRUST
Sweet tart pastry (see pages 8–9)

STRAWBERRY FILLING
1¹/₂ cups (450 g) whole fruit strawberry preserves (jam)
¹/₂ cup (80 g) sliced almonds

SERVES 8 · PREPARATION 30 MINUTES + 1 HOUR TO CHILL & COOL
COOKING 20-25 MINUTES

CRUST **1. Prepare** the sweet tart pastry and chill for at least 30 minutes. **2. Line** an 11-inch (28-cm) tart pan with a removable bottom with the pastry and bake blind following the instructions on page 9. Let cool a little while you prepare the filling.

FILLING **3. Preheat** the oven to 375°F (190°C/gas 5). **4. Spoon** the strawberry preserves into the baked pastry crust, spreading evenly with a spatula. Sprinkle the almonds over the top. **5. Bake** for 10 minutes, or until the preserves are bubbling and the almonds are light golden brown. **6. Serve** warm or at room temperature.

Try this classic tart that can be baked at any time of the year. You can vary the recipe by replacing the strawberry preserves with raspberry preserves.

● If you liked this recipe, try the chocolate Linzer torte on page 86.

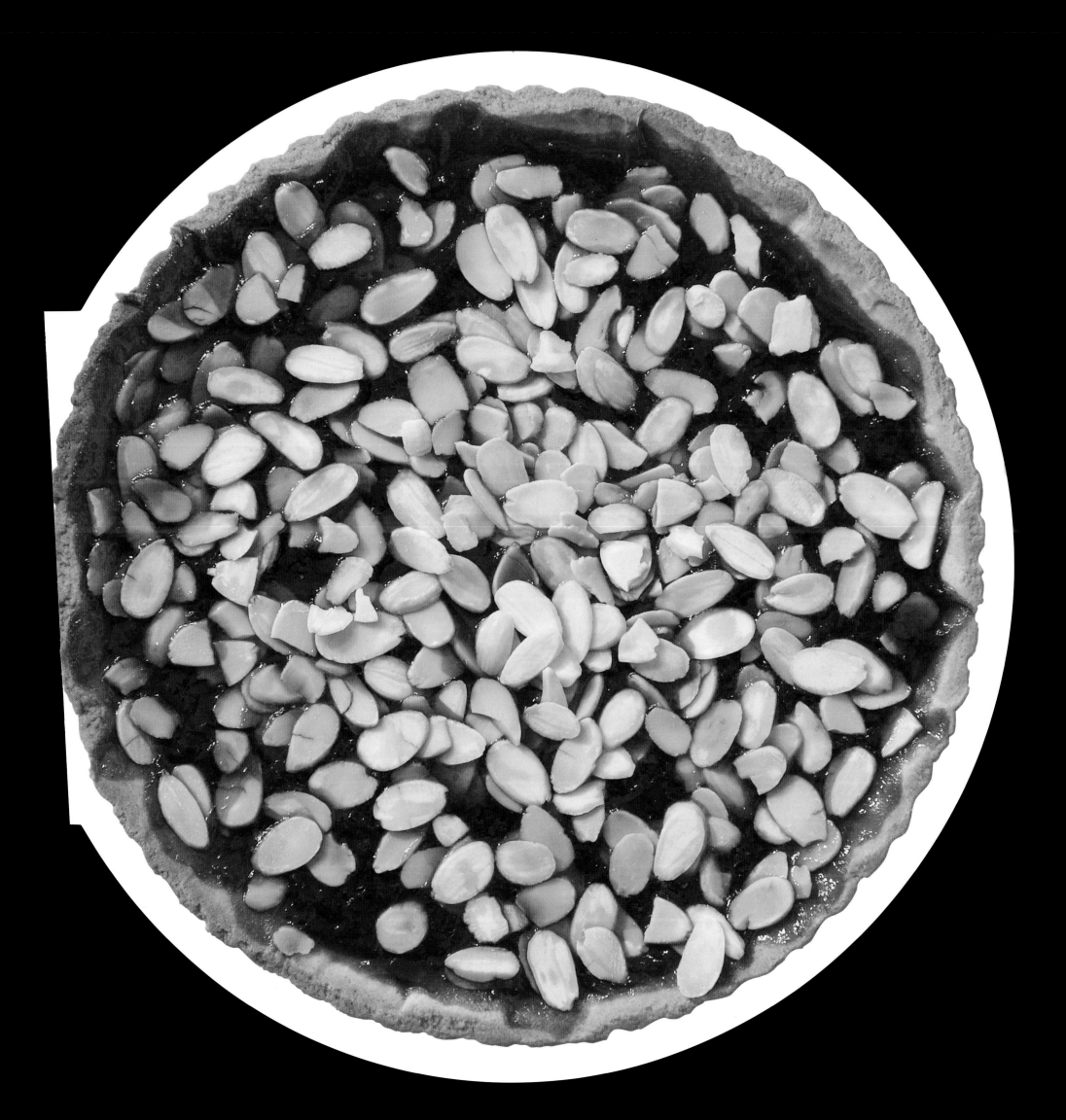

raspberry & custard tart

SERVES 8 • **PREPARATION** 30 MINUTES + 2 HOURS TO CHILL & COOL • **COOKING** 25-35 MINUTES

CRUST
Sweet tart pastry (see pages 8-9)

PASTRY CREAM
2 cups (500 ml) milk • ½ cinnamon stick • 3 large egg yolks
⅓ cup (75 g) sugar • 3 tablespoons cornstarch (cornflour) • 1 tablespoon salted butter

TOPPING
2-3 cups (300-450 g) fresh raspberries

CRUST **1. Prepare** the sweet tart pastry and chill for at least 30 minutes. **2. Line** an 11-inch (28-cm) tart pan with a removable bottom with the pastry and bake blind following the instructions on page 9. Let cool a little while you prepare the filling. PASTRY CREAM **3. Preheat** the oven to 400°F (230°C/gas 8). **4. Heat** the milk and cinnamon stick in a medium saucepan over medium heat and bring to a boil. Decrease the heat to very low, cover, and simmer gently for 5 minutes. **5. Strain** the milk through a fine mesh sieve into a pitcher (jug). **6. Beat** the egg yolks, sugar, and cornstarch in a medium bowl until combined. Gradually pour in the hot milk, stirring with a wooden spoon until incorporated. **7. Pour** the custard into a medium saucepan and simmer over low heat, stirring continuously with a wooden spoon until thickened. Remove from the heat, stir in the butter, and set aside to cool a little. TOPPING **8. Pour** the custard into the baked pastry crust and top with the raspberries. **9. Bake** for 10 minutes. **10. Serve** warm or at room temperature.

• **If you liked this recipe, try the chocolate raspberry pie on page 84.**

16

apple tart with calvados

SERVES 8 . PREPARATION 30 MINUTES + 1 HOUR TO CHILL . COOKING 45–55 MINUTES

CRUST

Sweet tart pastry (see pages 8–9)

FILLING

3 medium cooking apples, peeled, cored, and diced • 2 tablespoons granulated sugar • 1 tablespoon Calvados • 1 tablespoon salted butter ½ teaspoon ground cinnamon

TOPPING

2 medium cooking apples, peeled and cored • 1 tablespoon salted butter, melted • ¼ cup (50 g) granulated sugar 4 tablespoons confectioners' (icing) sugar • 3 tablespoons apricot preserves (jam) • 1 tablespoon Calvados (apple brandy)

CRUST **1. Prepare** the sweet tart pastry and chill for at least 30 minutes. **2. Line** an 11-inch (28-cm) tart pan with a removable bottom with the pastry and bake blind following the instructions on page 9. Let cool.

FILLING **3. Put** the apples in a medium saucepan. Add the granulated sugar, Calvados, butter, and cinnamon, and simmer over medium-low heat, stirring often, until softened, 10–15 minutes. Mash the apples and simmer over very low heat until most of the liquid has evaporated. **4. Spoon** the apple filling into the baked pastry crust and set aside.

TOPPING **5. Preheat** the oven to 375°F (190°C/gas 5). **6. Thinly slice** the apples lengthwise. Arrange over the filling in a circular pattern, starting from the center and working out to the edge of the tart. Brush with melted butter and sprinkle with the granulated sugar. **7. Bake** for 20 minutes, until the apples are tender. **8. Preheat** the broiler (grill) to high heat. **9. Dust** the tart with confectioners' sugar and cover the pastry edges with aluminum foil. Place the tart 4 inches (10 cm) from the heat source and broil until apples are golden, 1–2 minutes. Discard the foil. **10. Heat** the apricot preserves and Calvados in a small saucepan. Brush over the tart. **11. Serve** warm.

Calvados is an apple brandy made in Normandy. It is distilled from specially grown and selected apples.

• **If you liked this recipe,** try the apple pie on page 106.

orange ricotta
tart

CRUST

Sweet tart pastry (see pages 8–9)

FILLING

2 large eggs • 1 large egg yolk • 1½ cups (375 g) fresh ricotta cheese, drained
⅔ cup (100 g) confectioners' (icing) sugar • 2 teaspoons finely grated orange zest
1½ tablespoons Grand Marnier • 1 cup (250 ml) heavy (double) cream

SERVES 8 • PREPARATION 45 MINUTES + 1 HOUR TO CHILL & COOL
COOKING 30–40 MINUTES

CRUST **1. Prepare** the sweet tart pastry and chill for at least 30 minutes. **2. Line** an 11-inch (28-cm) tart pan with a removable bottom with the pastry and bake blind following the instructions on page 9. Let cool a little while you prepare the filling.

FILLING **3. Preheat** the oven to 375°F (190°C/gas 5). **4. Put** the eggs, egg yolk, ricotta, confectioners' sugar, orange zest, and Grand Marnier liqueur in a medium bowl and stir to combine. **5. Whip** ¾ cup (180 ml) of cream in a small bowl with an electric mixer on high speed until soft peaks form. **6. Fold** the cream into the ricotta mixture. **7. Spoon** into the baked pastry crust. **8. Bake** for 20–25 minutes, or until golden. **9. Let** cool to room temperature. **10. Whip** the remaining cream until thickened. Place in a pastry bag and decorate the top of the tart. **11. Serve** immediately.

Serve this tart in winter when oranges are in season. Be sure to choose organic oranges. These have not been treated with chemicals or wax.

● If you liked this recipe, try the lemon & lime meringue pie on page 32.

24

fruit tart

CRUST

Sweet tart pastry (see pages 8–9)

FILLING & TOPPING

5 ounces (150 g) cream cheese, softened • ½ cup (75 g) confectioners' (icing) sugar • 2 tablespoons double (heavy) cream • 1 teaspoon finely grated lemon zest • 1 tablespoon freshly squeezed lemon juice • 4 strawberries, sliced 3–4 kiwi fruit, peeled and sliced • 1 cup (200 g) blackberries • 1 cup (200 g) raspberries ½ cup (100 g) blueberries • ⅓ cup (100 g) apple jelly

SERVES 8 • **PREPARATION** 45 MINUTES + 1 HOUR TO CHILL • **COOKING** 10–15 MINUTES

26

CRUST **1. Prepare** the sweet tart pastry and chill for at least 30 minutes. **2. Line** an 11-inch (28-cm) tart pan with a removable bottom with the pastry and bake blind following the instructions on page 9. Let cool a little while you prepare the filling. FILLING **3. Beat** the cream cheese, confectioners' sugar, cream, lemon zest, and lemon juice until light and well blended. **4. Spread** evenly in the cooled baked pastry crust. **5. Arrange** a row of strawberry slices around the outside edge of the tart so that the tips of each slice extend beyond the crust. Lay the kiwi fruit slices over the strawberries to partially overlap them. Arrange a standing row of blackberries inside the circle of kiwi fruit slices. Arrange a standing row of raspberries inside the blackberries. Place the blueberries in the center of the tart, covering the filling. The fruit should cover the filling with concentric circles. **6. Heat** the apple jelly until liquid. Brush over the fruit. **7. Chill** in the refrigerator for at least 30 minutes before serving.

This striking tart is perfect for special occasions. You can vary the fresh fruit topping according to what is in season.

● **If you liked this recipe, try the raspberry & custard tart on page 16.**

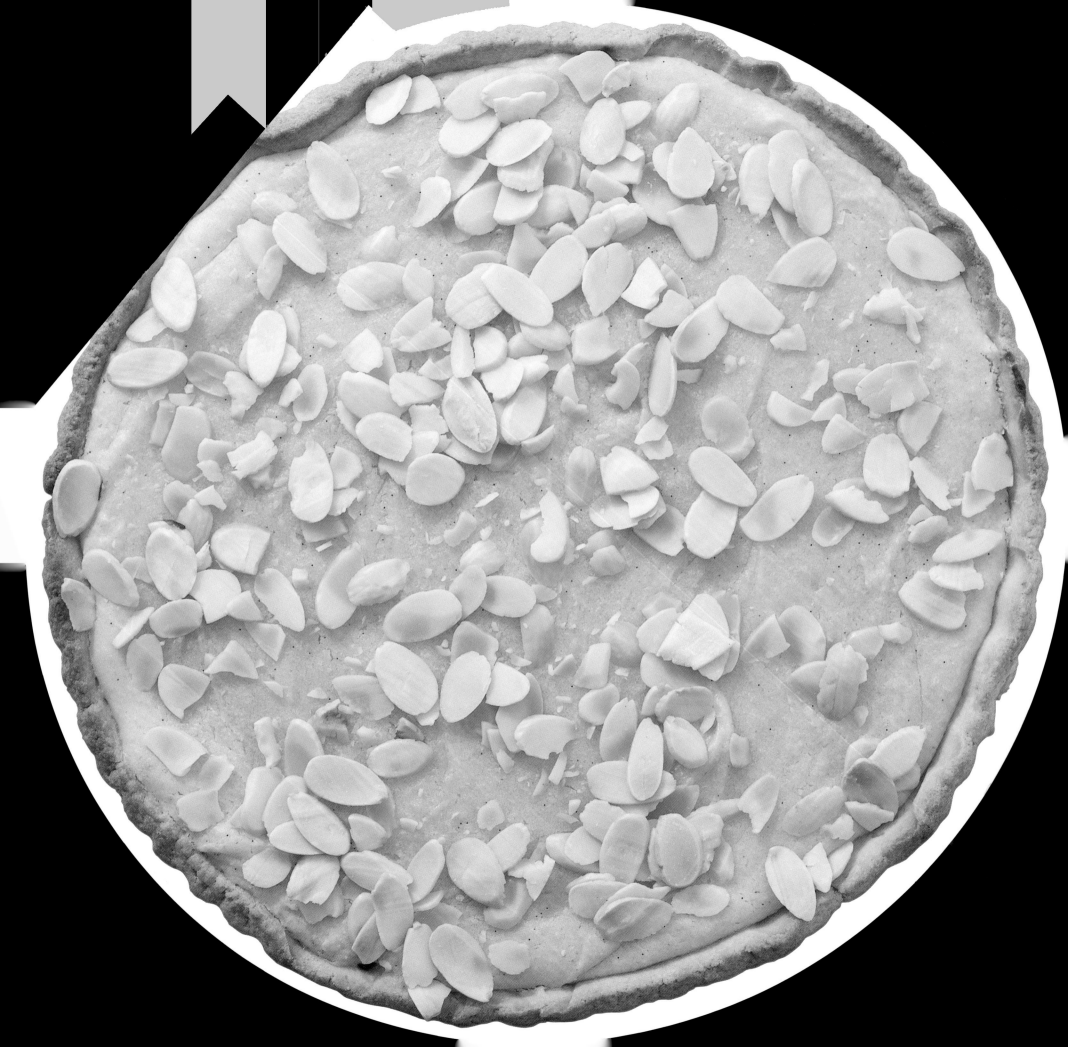

pine nut tart

CRUST

Sweet tart pastry (see pages 8–9)

PINE NUT FILLING

³/4 cup (180 ml) light corn (golden) syrup • 1¼ tablespoons freshly squeezed lemon juice • 3/4 cup (180 g) salted butter, softened • 3/4 cup (150 g) firmly packed light brown sugar • 1 teaspoon vanilla extract (essence) • 1 teaspoon finely grated lemon zest • 4 large eggs • 2 cups (350 g) pine nuts, lightly toasted

SERVES 8 • **PREPARATION** 30 MINUTES + 30 MINUTES TO CHILL • **COOKING** 45–55 MINUTES

CRUST 1. Prepare the sweet tart pastry and chill for at least 30 minutes. **2. Line** an 11-inch (28-cm) tart pan with a removable bottom with the pastry and bake blind following the instructions on page 9. Let cool a little while you prepare the filling.

FILLING 3. Preheat the oven to 350°F (180°/gas 4). **4. Heat** the corn syrup and lemon juice in a small saucepan over low heat until liquid. **5. Beat** the butter, brown sugar, vanilla, and lemon zest in a medium bowl with an electric mixer on medium-high speed until pale and creamy. Add the eggs one at a time, beating until just combined after each addition. Stir in the pine nuts with a wooden spoon. **6. Spoon** the filling into the baked pastry crust and bake for 35–40 minutes, until golden brown. **7. Serve** warm or at room temperature.

Pine nuts are full of protein and packed with vitamins and minerals. This tart is a superb way to enjoy the health benefits they bring!

• **If you liked this recipe, try the** blackberry & hazelnut streusel tart on page 44.

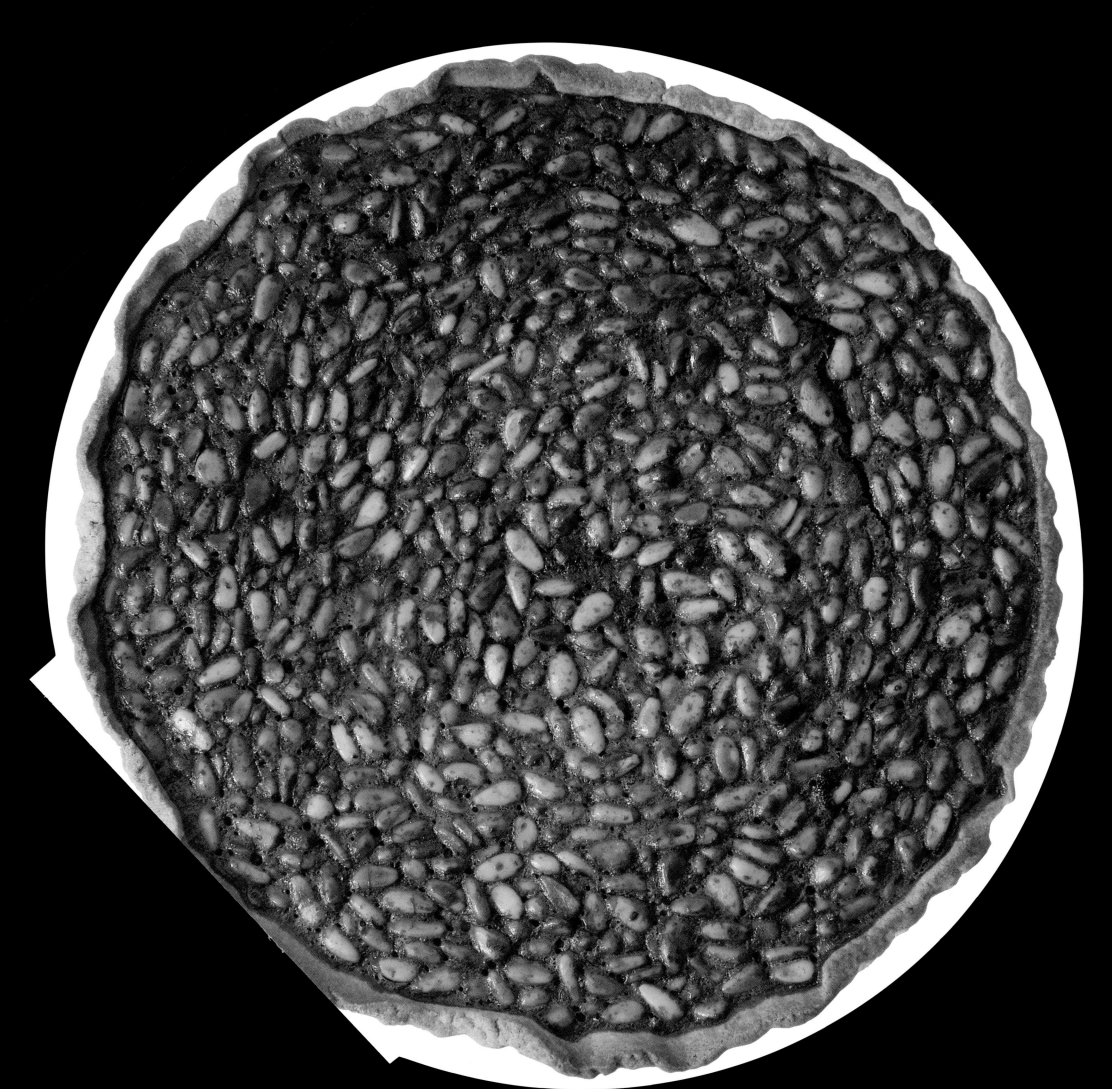

lemon & lime
meringue pie

CRUST
Sweet tart pastry (see pages 8–9)

FILLING & TOPPING
1 cup (200 g) superfine (caster) sugar · ¼ cup (60 ml) freshly squeezed lemon juice · ¼ cup (60 ml) freshly squeezed lime juice · 2 teaspoons finely grated lime zest · 2 teaspoons finely grated lemon zest · 6 large eggs, separated
½ cup (125 g) cold unsalted butter, cubed · ½ teaspoon vanilla extract (essence)

SERVES 8 · **PREPARATION** 45 MINUTES + 1 HOUR TO CHILL & COOL · **COOKING** 30–40 MINUTES

CRUST **1. Prepare** the sweet tart pastry and chill for at least 30 minutes. **2. Line** an 11-inch (28-cm) tart pan with a removable bottom with the pastry and bake blind following the instructions on page 9. Let cool a little while you prepare the filling.

FILLING **3. Preheat** the oven to 375°F (190°C/gas 5). **4. Stir** ½ cup (100 g) of superfine sugar with the lemon juice, lime juice, and both zests in a small saucepan over medium heat until the sugar has dissolved. **5. Beat** the egg yolks in a heatproof bowl and gradually add the hot citrus liquid. Strain the mixture through a fine-mesh sieve. Return to the bowl and place over a pan of

barely simmering water. Cook, stirring constantly, until the mixture thickens enough to coat the back of a wooden spoon. Do not allow it to boil. **6. Remove** from the heat and stir in the butter cubes one at a time. **7. Pour** the mixture into the baked pastry crust. **8. Beat** the egg whites with an electric mixer on medium speed until soft peaks form. Gradually add the remaining superfine sugar, beating until thick and glossy. Stir in the vanilla. **9. Spoon** over the filling, using a spatula to create wavelike peaks. **10. Bake** for 5–10 minutes, until the meringue is pale golden brown. **11. Cool** to room temperature before serving.

• If you liked this recipe, try the chocolate meringue pie on page 78.

tarte au chocolat

CRUST

Sweet tart pastry (see pages 8–9)

FILLING

2 cups (500 ml) heavy (double) cream · 14 ounces (400 g) dark chocolate (70% cacao), grated · 1 tablespoon Cointreau or brandy
1 cup (150 g) fresh raspberries, to serve

SERVES 8 · **PREPARATION** 30 MINUTES + 2 HOURS 45 MINUTES TO CHILL & COOL
COOKING 20-25 MINUTES

CRUST **1. Prepare** the sweet tart pastry and chill for at least 30 minutes. **2. Line** an 11-inch (28-cm) tart pan with a removable bottom with the pastry and bake blind following the instructions on page 9. Let cool. FILLING **3. Pour** the cream into a heavy saucepan and bring slowly to a boil. As soon as the first bubbles appear, remove from the heat and stir in the chocolate. Add the Cointreau and stir until all the chocolate has melted. Whisk until smooth, then let cool for 15 minutes. **4. Pour** the filling into the baked pastry crust and chill in the refrigerator for 2 hours. **5. Serve** with the raspberries.

If you are preparing this classic tart ahead of time, you can make and bake the pastry crust the day before. But don't prepare and fill the tart until 3–4 hours before serving.

● **If you liked this recipe,** try the cool chocolate macadamia tart on page 80.

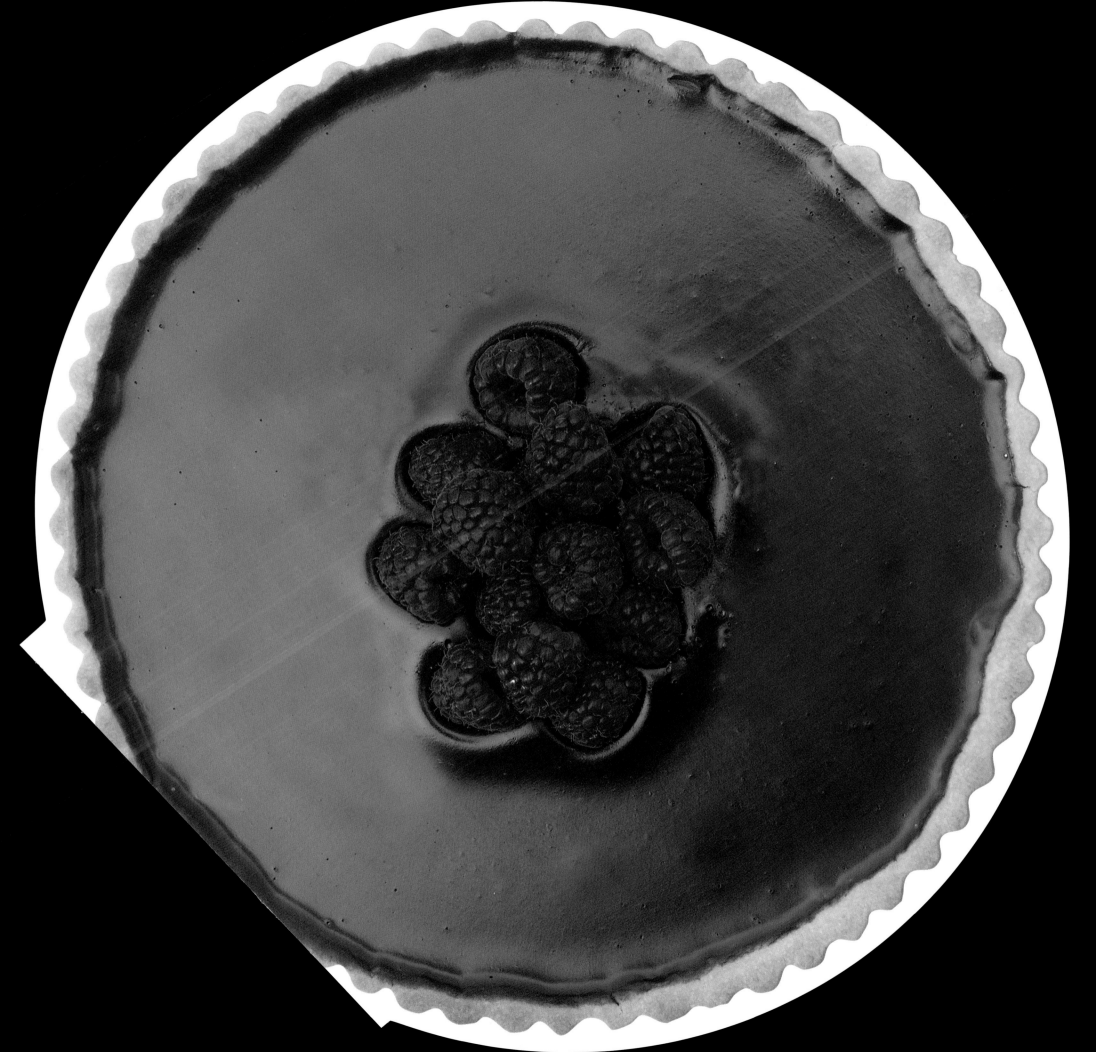

CRUST

Sweet tart pastry (see pages 8–9),
made with 1 teaspoon finely grated lemon zest

CUSTARD FILLING

3 large eggs + 2 large egg yolks · 3 tablespoons superfine (caster) sugar · 2 cups
(500 ml) heavy cream · 1½ cups (375 ml) milk · 1 teaspoon freshly ground nutmeg

SERVES 8 · PREPARATION 30 MINUTES + 2 HOURS TO CHILL & COOL
COOKING 55–65 MINUTES

custard tart
with nutmeg

CRUST 1. Prepare the sweet tart pastry, adding the lemon zest with the other ingredients. Chill the pastry for at least 30 minutes. 2. Line an 11-inch (28-cm) tart pan with a removable bottom with the pastry and bake blind following the instructions on page 9. Let cool a little while you prepare the filling.

FILLING 3. Preheat the oven to 350°F (180°C/gas 4). 4. Whisk the eggs, egg yolks, sugar, cream, and milk in a medium bowl until combined. Pour the egg mixture into the baked pastry crust. 5. Bake for 45–50 minutes or until just set. Remove from the oven and dust the top with the nutmeg. 6. Let cool to room temperature. Chill in the refrigerator for at least 1 hour before serving.

A slice of custard tart is the ultimate comfort food. Serve as is or with sliced fresh fruit.

● **If you liked this recipe, try the almond custard tart on page 28.**

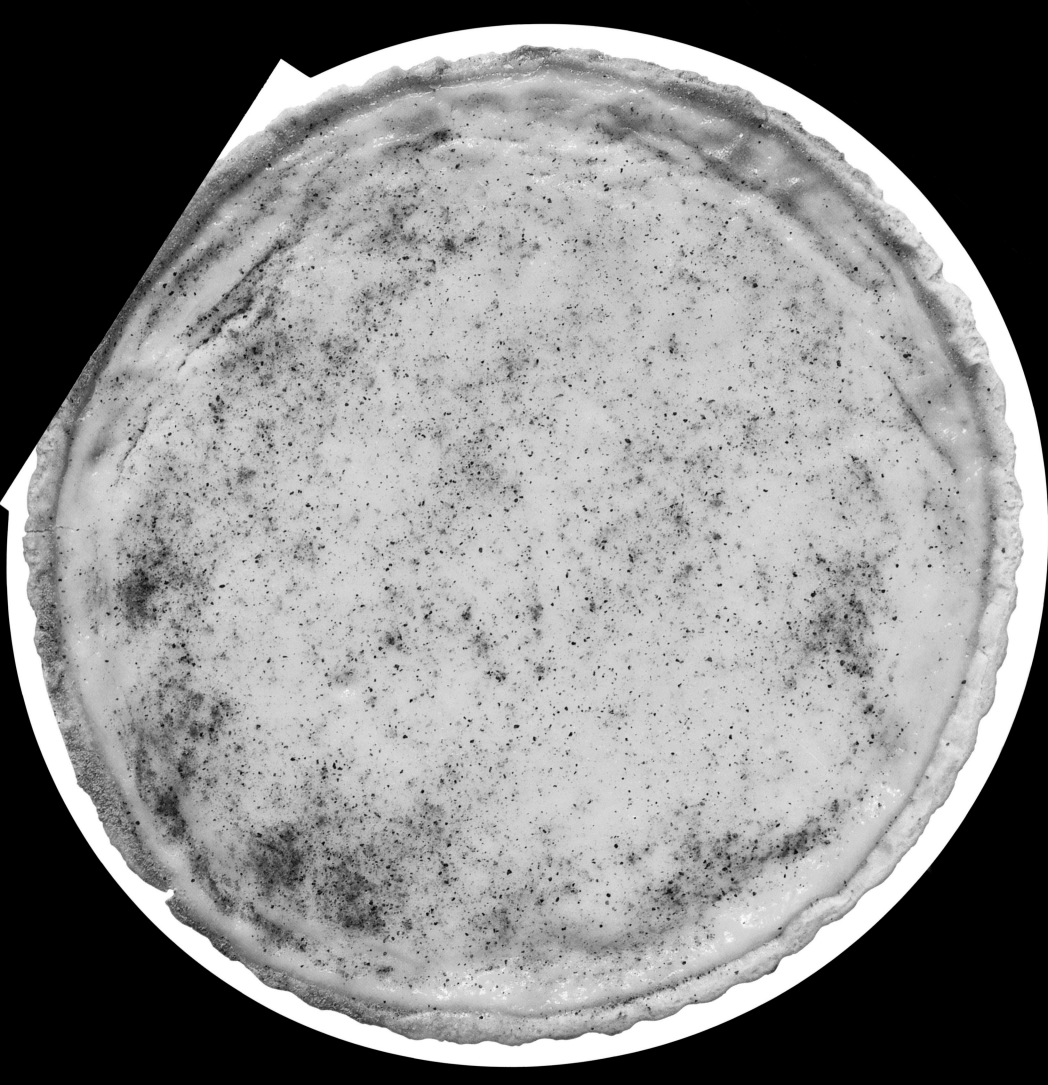

coconut & mango
tart

CRUST

Sweet tart pastry (see pages 8–9)

COCONUT & MANGO FILLING

4 large eggs • 1 1/2 cups (300 g) superfine (caster) sugar • 1 cup (250 g) mascarpone cheese • 3/4 cup (180 ml) coconut milk • 2 cups (300 g) shredded (desiccated) coconut • 2 fresh or canned mangos, sliced lengthwise

SERVES 8 • PREPARATION 30 MINUTES + 1 HOUR 30 MINUTES TO CHILL

COOKING 50–55 MINUTES

CRUST 1. **Prepare** the sweet tart pastry and chill for at least 30 minutes. 2. **Line** an 11-inch (28-cm) tart pan with a removable bottom with the pastry and bake blind following the instructions on page 9. Let cool a little while you prepare the filling. FILLING 3. **Preheat** the oven to 350°F (180°C/gas 4). 4. **Beat** the eggs and superfine sugar with an electric mixer on medium-high speed until light and fluffy. Stir in the mascarpone, coconut milk, and coconut by hand until well combined. 5. **Spoon** the filling into the baked pastry crust. Arrange the mango slices on the top fanning out like the spokes of a bicycle wheel. 6. **Bake** for 40 minutes or until golden brown. 7. **Let cool** and set for 1 hour before serving.

Mangoes are not only delicious, they are also an excellent source of carotenes and vitamin C.

• If you liked this recipe, try the raspberry & coconut pie on page 108.

CRUST
Sweet tart pastry (see pages 8–9)

FRANGIPANE FILLING
1 cup (200 g) superfine (caster) sugar • 3/4 cup (180 g) unsalted butter, softened • 1/2 cup (75 g) all-purpose (plain) flour • 1 1/2 cups (225 g) ground almonds • 4 large eggs • 1 teaspoon almond extract (essence) • 1/2 cup (150 g) strawberry preserves (jam) • 1/2 cup (50 g) sliced almonds

SERVES 8 • **PREPARATION** 30 MINUTES + 1 HOUR TO CHILL & COOL
COOKING 45-55 MINUTES

40

Bakewell tart

CRUST **1. Prepare** the sweet tart pastry and chill for at least 30 minutes. **2. Line** an 11-inch (28-cm) tart pan with a removable bottom with the pastry and bake blind following the instructions on page 9. Let cool a little while you prepare the filling. FILLING **3. Preheat** the oven to 325°F (170°C/gas 3). **4. Process** the superfine sugar, butter, flour, ground almonds, eggs, and almond extract in a food processor until a smooth, paste is formed, about 2 minutes. **5. Spread** the strawberry preserves over the baked pastry crust and spoon the frangipane mixture on top, smoothing the surface with a spatula or the back of a spoon. **6. Bake** for 30 minutes. Remove from the oven, sprinkle with sliced almonds and bake for 5–10 more minutes, until golden brown. **7. Serve** at room temperature.

A Bakewell tart is a traditional English dessert, said to have been created in the 1860s in the village of Bakewell in Derbyshire.

● If you liked this recipe, try the almond custard tart on page 28.

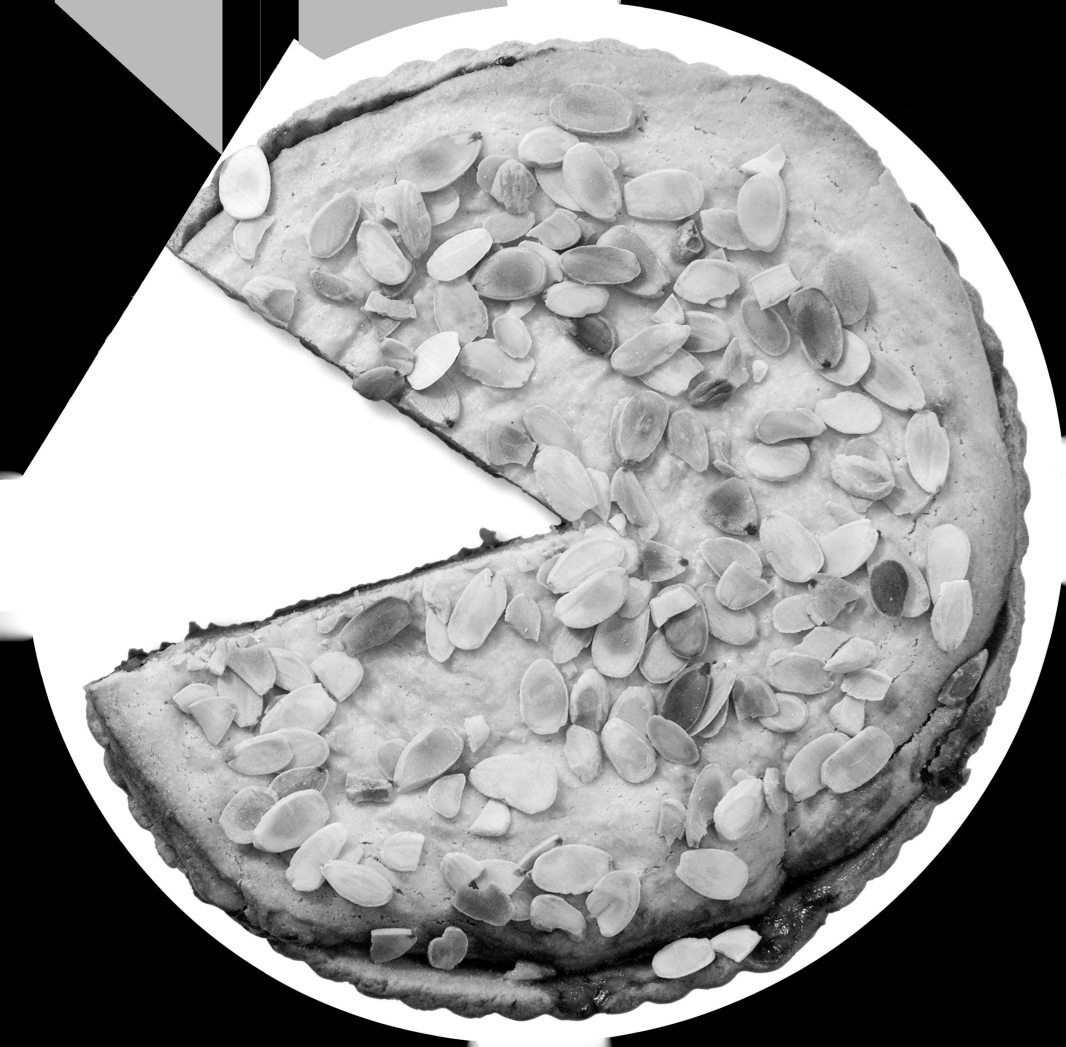

CRUST

Sweet tart pastry (see pages 8–9)

APPLE & PECAN FILLING

¹/₄ cup (60 ml) Calvados or other apple brandy · 6 tablespoons Demerara sugar · ¹/₂ vanilla bean, split lengthwise and seeds scraped ¹/₂ teaspoon ground cinnamon · 6 Granny Smith apples, peeled, cored, and quartered 1 cup (120 g) pecans · Whipped cream, to serve

SERVES 8 · PREPARATION 45 MINUTES + 30 MINUTES TO CHILL · COOKING 45–65 MINUTES

apple & pecan
tart

CRUST **1. Prepare** the sweet tart pastry and chill for at least 30 minutes. **2. Line** an 11-inch (28-cm) tart pan with a removable bottom with the pastry and bake blind following the instructions on page 9. Let cool a little while you prepare the filling.
FILLING **3. Preheat** the oven to 350°F (180°C/gas 4). **4. Combine** the Calvados, Demerara sugar, vanilla bean and seeds, and cinnamon in a large saucepan over medium-low heat and simmer until the sugar has dissolved. **5. Add** the apples and simmer, stirring often, until the apples have softened a little, 5–10 minutes. Stir in the pecans. **6. Arrange** the apple quarters decoratively in the baked pastry shell. Remove the vanilla bean from the syrup and pour over the apples. **7. Bake** for 30–40 minutes, until the apples are pale gold and tender. **8. Serve** warm or at room temperature with a dollop whipped cream.

This tart is also good served hot with vanilla ice cream.

● **If you liked this recipe, try the apple & blueberry pie on page 110.**

42

ricotta & plum tart

CRUST

Sweet tart pastry (see pages 8–9)

RICOTTA & PLUM FILLING

1 cup (250 g) mascarpone cheese • 1¼ cups (300 g) fresh ricotta cheese, drained • ¾ cup (150 g) granulated sugar • ½ cup (125 ml) honey 1½ teaspoons vanilla extract (essence) • 3 large eggs + 1 large egg yolk • 2 tablespoons all-purpose (plain) flour • 15 ripe plums, pitted and quartered • 4 tablespoons apricot preserves (jam)

SERVES 8 • PREPARATION 30 MINUTES + 30 MINUTES TO CHILL • COOKING 40–55 MINUTES

CRUST **1. Prepare** the sweet tart pastry and chill for at least 30 minutes. **2. Line** an 11-inch (28-cm) tart pan with a removable bottom with the pastry and bake blind following the instructions on page 9. Let cool a little while you prepare the filling. FILLING **3. Preheat** the oven to 325°F (170°C/ gas 3). **4. Beat** the mascarpone, ricotta, sugar, honey, and vanilla in a medium bowl with an electric mixer on medium speed until smooth. Beat in the eggs, egg yolk, and flour until well combined. **5. Spoon** into the baked pastry crust. Arrange the plum quarters around the tart decoratively. **6. Bake** for 30–40 minutes, until the filling is light golden brown but still slightly wobbly. **7. Heat** the apricot preserves in a small saucepan over low heat. **8. Brush** over the tart and serve warm.

For best results, choose a slightly tart, ripe red plum for this recipe. The tang of the fruit will contrast beautifully with the sweet and creamy cheese filling.

● If you liked this recipe, try the orange ricotta tart on page 24.

46

plum & amaretti crunch tart

CRUST

Sweet tart pastry (see pages 8–9)

PLUM FILLING

3 tablespoons ground almonds · 2 tablespoons dark brown sugar

2 teaspoons finely grated orange zest · 3/4 cup (180 g) mascarpone cheese

12–15 plums, peeled, halved, and pitted

AMARETTI TOPPING

1/2 cup (125 g) salted butter, softened · 6 tablespoons firmly packed light brown sugar

2 cups (200 g) crushed amaretti cookies · 2/3 cup (100 g) flaked almonds · 6 tablespoons shredded

(desiccated) coconut · 2 teaspoons ground cinnamon

SERVES 8 · PREPARATION 40 MINUTES + 30 MINUTES TO CHILL · COOKING 45–55 MINUTES

CRUST **1. Prepare** the sweet tart pastry and chill for at least 30 minutes. **2. Line** an 11-inch (28-cm) tart pan with a removable bottom with the pastry and bake blind, following the instructions on page 9. Let cool a little while you prepare the filling and topping.

FILLING **3. Preheat** the oven to 375°F (190°C/gas 5). **4. Combine** the almonds, brown sugar, orange zest, and mascarpone in a medium bowl, stirring with a wooden spoon. Add the plum halves, stirring to coat in the mascarpone mixture. **5. Spoon** into the baked pastry crust.

TOPPING **6. Put** all the topping ingredients in a medium bowl and rub together using your fingertips until combined into a lumpy mixture. **7. Sprinkle** the topping over the plum-filled tart. **8. Bake** for 35–40 minutes, until the topping is golden brown. **9. Serve** warm or at room temperature.

This fruity tart is especially good served with warm, creamy custard or a scoop or two of homemade vanilla ice cream.

● **If you liked this recipe,** try the blackberry & hazelnut streusel tart on page 44.

passion fruit tart

CRUST

Sweet tart pastry (see pages 8–9)

PASSION FRUIT FILLING

1³/4 cups (350 g) superfine (caster) sugar · 1¹/4 cups (300 ml) passion fruit pulp, strained · 1 tablespoon freshly squeezed orange juice · 1 teaspoon finely grated orange zest · 7 large egg yolks · 1¹/4 cups (300 g) unsalted butter, cubed

SERVES 8 · **PREPARATION** 30 MINUTES + 1 HOUR 30 MINUTES TO CHILL

COOKING 15–20 MINUTES

CRUST **1. Prepare** the sweet tart pastry and chill for at least 30 minutes. **2. Line** an 11-inch (28-cm) tart pan with a removable bottom with the pastry and bake blind following the instructions on page 9. Let cool a little while you prepare the filling.

FILLING **3. Heat** the sugar, passion fruit pulp, orange juice, and zest in a small saucepan over medium heat, stirring until the sugar has dissolved. **4. Beat** the eggs yolks in a heatproof bowl and gradually pour in the hot passion fruit mixture. Strain through a fine-mesh sieve. Return to the heatproof bowl and place over a saucepan of barely simmering water. Cook, stirring continuously, until the mixture thickens and coats the back of a wooden spoon. Do not allow the mixture to boil. **5. Remove** from the heat and add the butter, one cube at a time, whisking until fully incorporated. **6. Pour** the passion fruit curd into the baked pastry crust and smooth using a spatula or the back of a spoon. **7. Chill** in the refrigerator for at least 1 hour before serving.

This elegant tart is chilled before serving; be sure not to chill for more than 3–4 hours or the pastry will become soggy and unappetizing.

● **If you liked this recipe, try the lemon tart on page 12.**

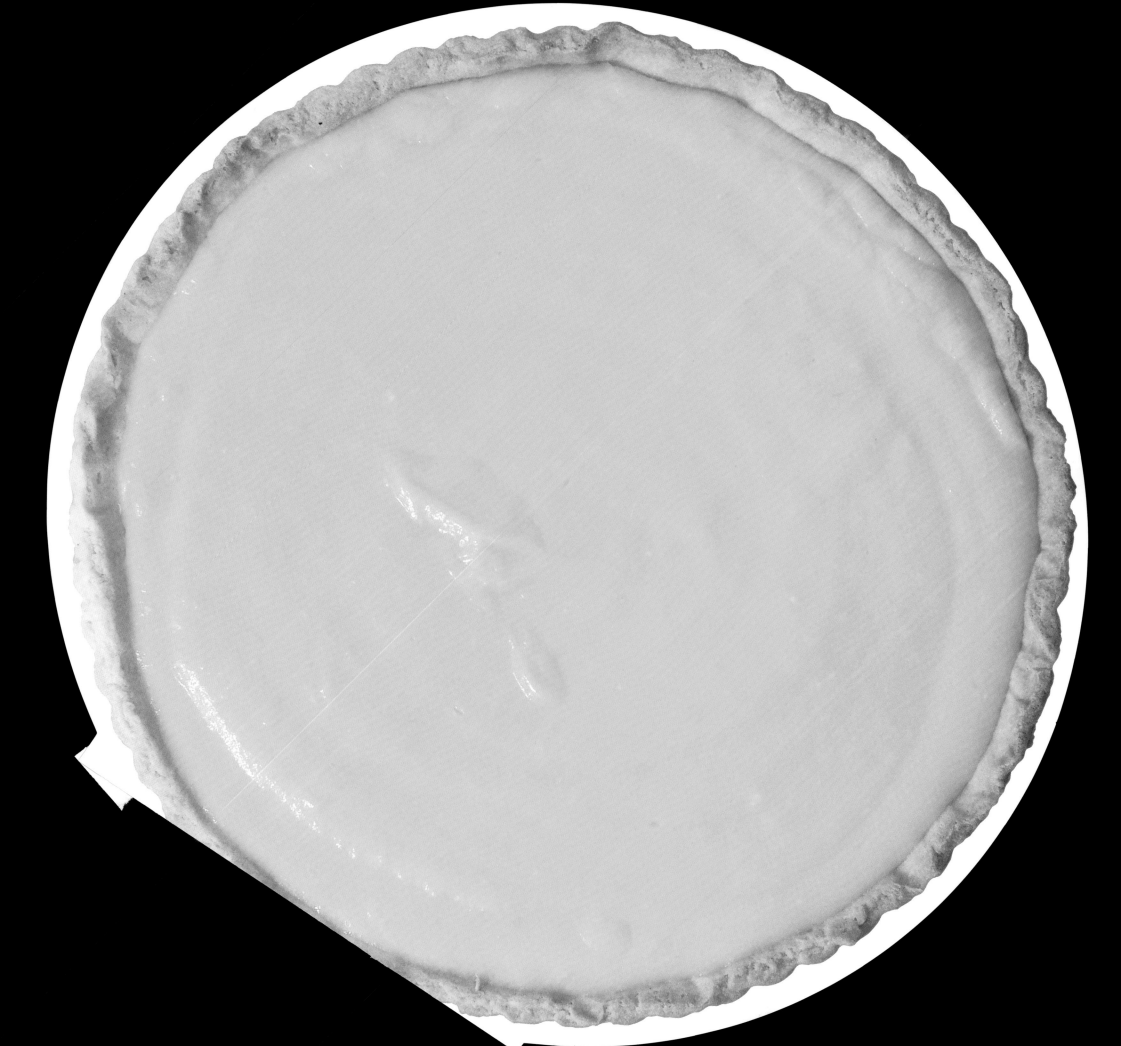

mochaccino tart

CRUST
Chocolate sweet tart pastry (see pages 8–9)

MOCHA FILLING
14 ounces (400 g) dark chocolate, coarsely chopped · 1½ cups (375 ml) heavy (double) cream · ¼ cup (60 ml) coffee liqueur
1 tablespoon freeze-dried coffee granules

TOPPING
1 cup (250 ml) heavy (double) cream · ⅓ cup (90 g) mascarpone cheese
3 tablespoons confectioners' (icing) sugar · Unsweetened cocoa powder, to dust

SERVES 8 · PREPARATION 40 MINUTES + 1 HOUR 30 MINUTES TO CHILL · COOKING 15–20 MINUTES

CRUST **1. Prepare** the chocolate sweet tart pastry and chill for at least 30 minutes. **2. Line** an 11-inch (28-cm) tart pan with a removable bottom with the pastry and bake blind following the instructions on page 9. Let cool a little while you prepare the filling. FILLING **3. Heat** the chocolate, cream, coffee liqueur, and coffee granules in the top of a double boiler over barely simmering water, stirring occasionally, until smooth. **4. Pour** the filling into the baked pastry crust and chill in the refrigerator until set, about 1 hour. TOPPING **5. Beat** the cream, mascarpone, and confectioners' sugar with an electric mixer on medium speed until soft peaks form. **6. Spread** the cream mixture on top of the tart and dust with cocoa. **7. Serve** immediately.

Serve this rich and creamy tart for dessert with tiny cups of espresso.

• If you liked this recipe, try the rich mocha pie on page 82.

crème brûlée tart

CRUST

Sweet tart pastry (see pages 8–9)

FILLING

7 large egg yolks · 3/4 cup (150 g) + 5 tablespoons superfine (caster) sugar
1 3/4 cups (450 ml) heavy (double) cream · 3/4 cup (180 ml) milk
1 vanilla bean, split lengthwise and seeds scraped out

SERVES 8 · PREPARATION 50 MINUTES + 3 HOURS TO CHILL & COOL
COOKING 50–60 MINUTES

CRUST **1. Prepare** the sweet tart pastry and chill for at least 30 minutes. **2. Line** an 11-inch (28-cm) tart pan with a removable bottom with the pastry and bake blind, following the instructions on page 9. Let cool a little while you prepare the filling.

FILLING **3. Preheat** the oven to 325°F (170°C/gas 3). **4. Beat** the egg yolks and 3/4 cup (150 g) of superfine sugar in a medium bowl until pale and creamy. **5. Heat** the cream, milk, and vanilla bean and seeds in a small saucepan over medium-high heat and bring to a boil. **6. Gradually pour** the hot cream mixture into the egg yolks, whisking until incorporated. Strain the custard through a fine-mesh sieve, discarding the vanilla. **7. Pour** the custard into the baked pastry crust. **8. Bake** for 35–40 minutes, until set. **9. Let cool** to room temperature in the pan. Refrigerate for 1 hour, until chilled and set. **10. Preheat** the broiler (grill) to high. **11. Sprinkle** the tart with the 5 tablespoons of remaining superfine sugar. Cover the pastry edges with foil to prevent them from burning. **12. Place** the tart on the highest shelf underneath the broiler and broil until the sugar caramelizes and turns golden brown, 1–2 minutes. **13. Serve** immediately.

For a richer flavor, substitute the superfine sugar in the topping with the same quantity of brown sugar.

● **If you liked this recipe, try the custard tart with nutmeg on page 36.**

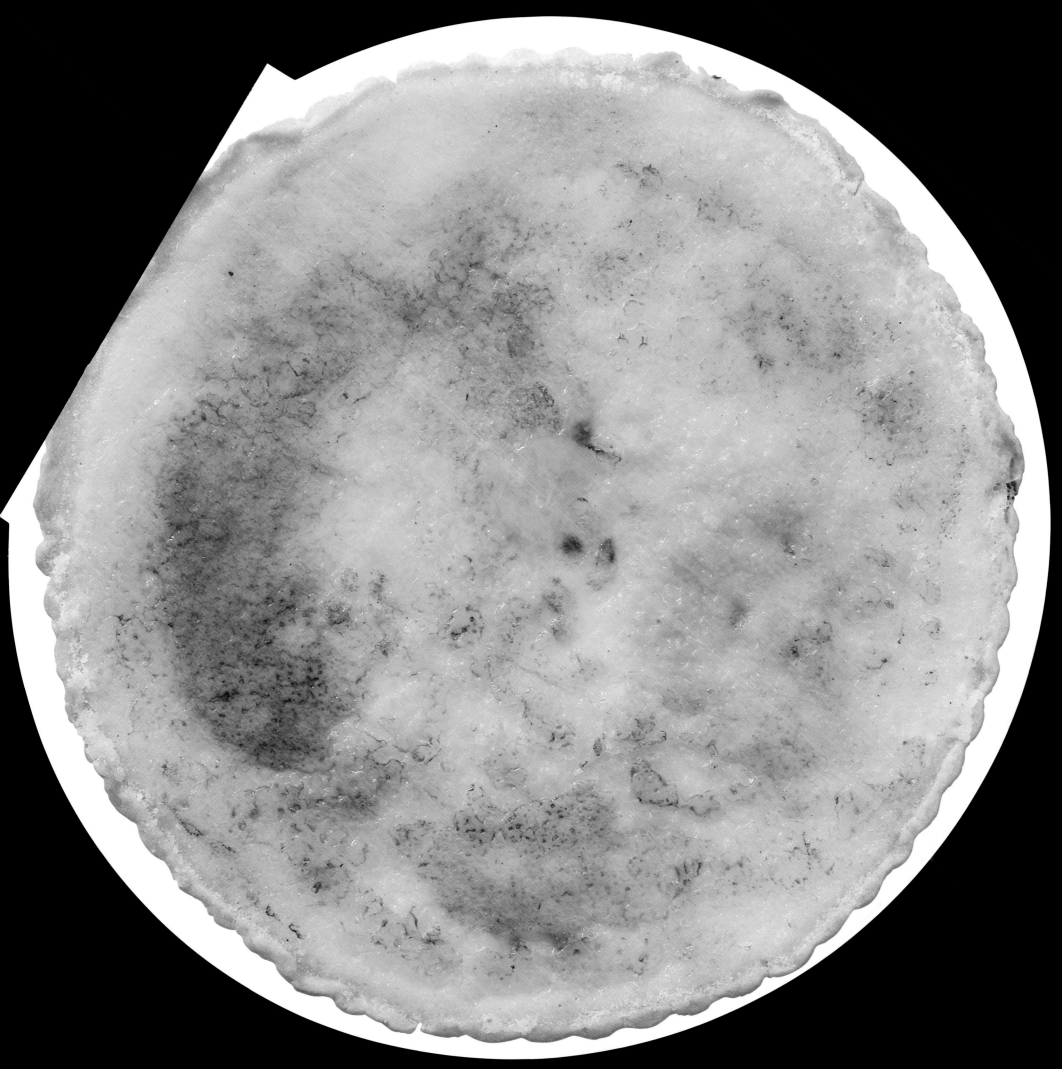

tiramisu tart

SERVES 8 · PREPARATION 30 MINUTES + 2 HOURS 30 MINUTES TO CHILL · COOKING 10–15 MINUTES

CRUST

Sweet tart pastry (see pages 8–9)

FILLING

2 cups (500 g) mascarpone cheese · 3/4 cup (180 ml) heavy (double) cream
3/4 cup (150 g) superfine (caster) sugar · 3/4 cup (180 ml) strong, dark espresso
1/3 cup (90 ml) amaretto (almond liqueur) · 12–16 ladyfinger cookies
3 ounces (90 g) dark chocolate, finely grated

CRUST **1. Prepare** the sweet tart pastry and chill for at least 30 minutes. **2. Line** an 11-inch (28-cm) tart pan with a removable bottom with the pastry and bake blind, following the instructions on page 9. Let the tart shell cool for 30 minutes. FILLING **3. Beat** the mascarpone, cream, and superfine sugar in a medium bowl with an electric mixer fitted with a whisk until stiff peaks form. **4. Spread** one-third of the cream mixture in the baked pastry crust. **5. Combine** the espresso and amaretto in a small bowl. Soak the ladyfingers in the mixture for a few seconds, then arrange on top of the cream layer. Spoon the remaining cream over the top and use a spatula or the back of a spoon to create a smooth surface. **6. Chill** in the refrigerator for 2 hours. **7. Sprinkle** with the chocolate just before serving.

Here's a new twist on an old favorite! Be sure to use a deep tart pan that will hold all the creamy filling.

• **If you liked this recipe, try** the divine mousse pie on page 74.

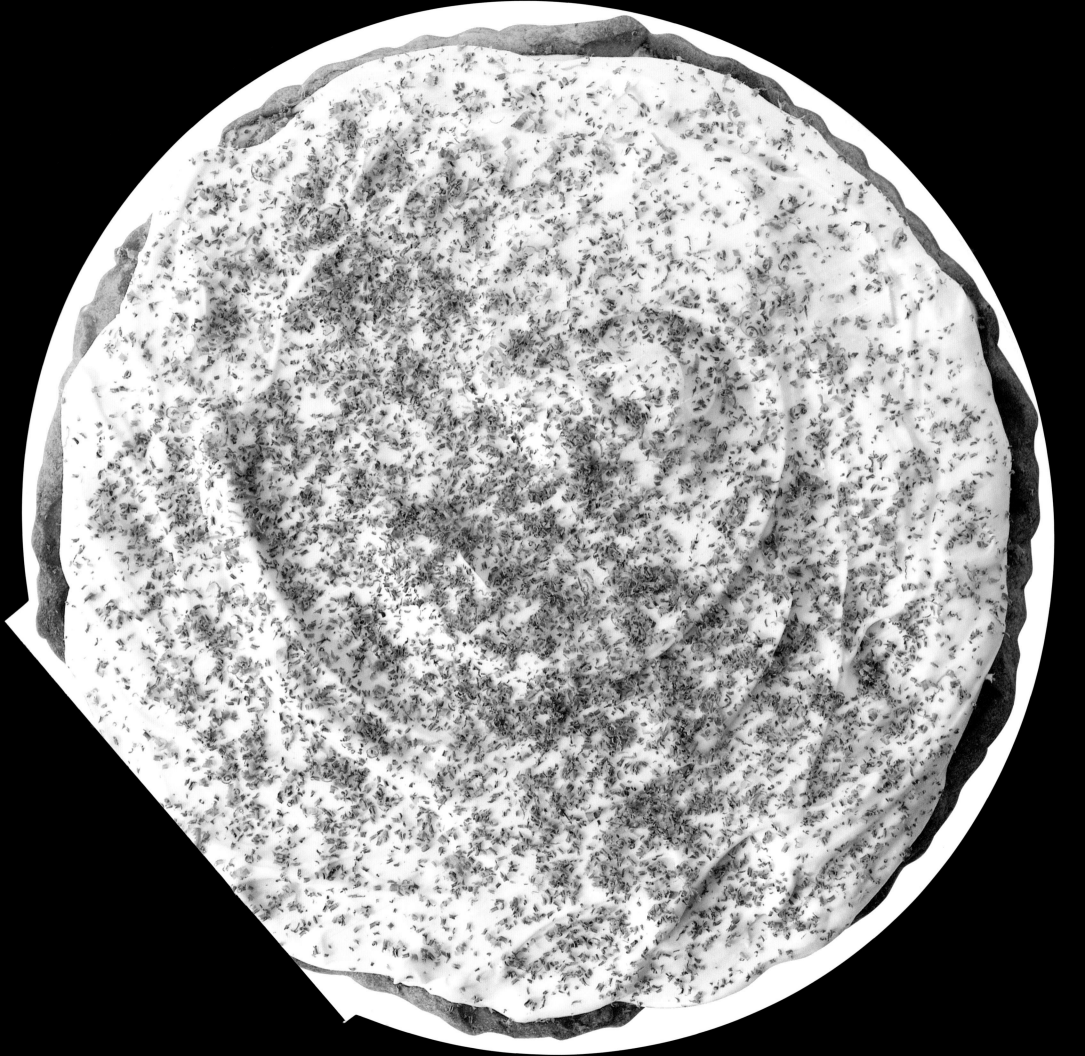

key lime pie

CRUST

Sweet tart pastry (see pages 8–9)

FILLING

3/4 cup (180 ml) freshly squeezed lime juice • 1 tablespoon unflavored gelatin powder • 4 large egg yolks • 1 (14-ounce/400-g) can sweetened condensed milk 1 tablespoon finely grated lime zest 1 cup (250 ml) heavy (double) cream

SERVES 8 • PREPARATION 30 MINUTES + 3 HOURS 30 MINUTES TO CHILL COOKING 20-25 MINUTES

CRUST 1. Prepare the sweet tart pastry and chill for at least 30 minutes. 2. Line an 11-inch (28-cm) tart pan with a removable bottom with the pastry and bake blind following the instructions on page 9. Let cool a little while you prepare the filling.

FILLING 3. Put the lime juice in a small saucepan and sprinkle with the gelatin. Set aside to soak for 5 minutes. 4. Beat the egg yolks in a medium bowl with an electric mixer on high speed until pale and thick. 5. Stir the lime juice and gelatin mixture over low heat until the gelatin is dissolved. 6. Add the condensed milk, lime juice mixture, and 1 teaspoon of the lime zest to the egg yolks, stirring well to combine. 7. Pour the filling into the baked pastry crust. 8. Chill in the refrigerator until set, about 3 hours. 9. Whip the cream in a small bowl with until soft peaks form. Spoon over the filling and sprinkle with the remaining 2 teaspoons lime zest. 10. Serve immediately.

You can also omit the cream topping for a lighter pie.

● If you liked this recipe, try the lemon tart on page 12.

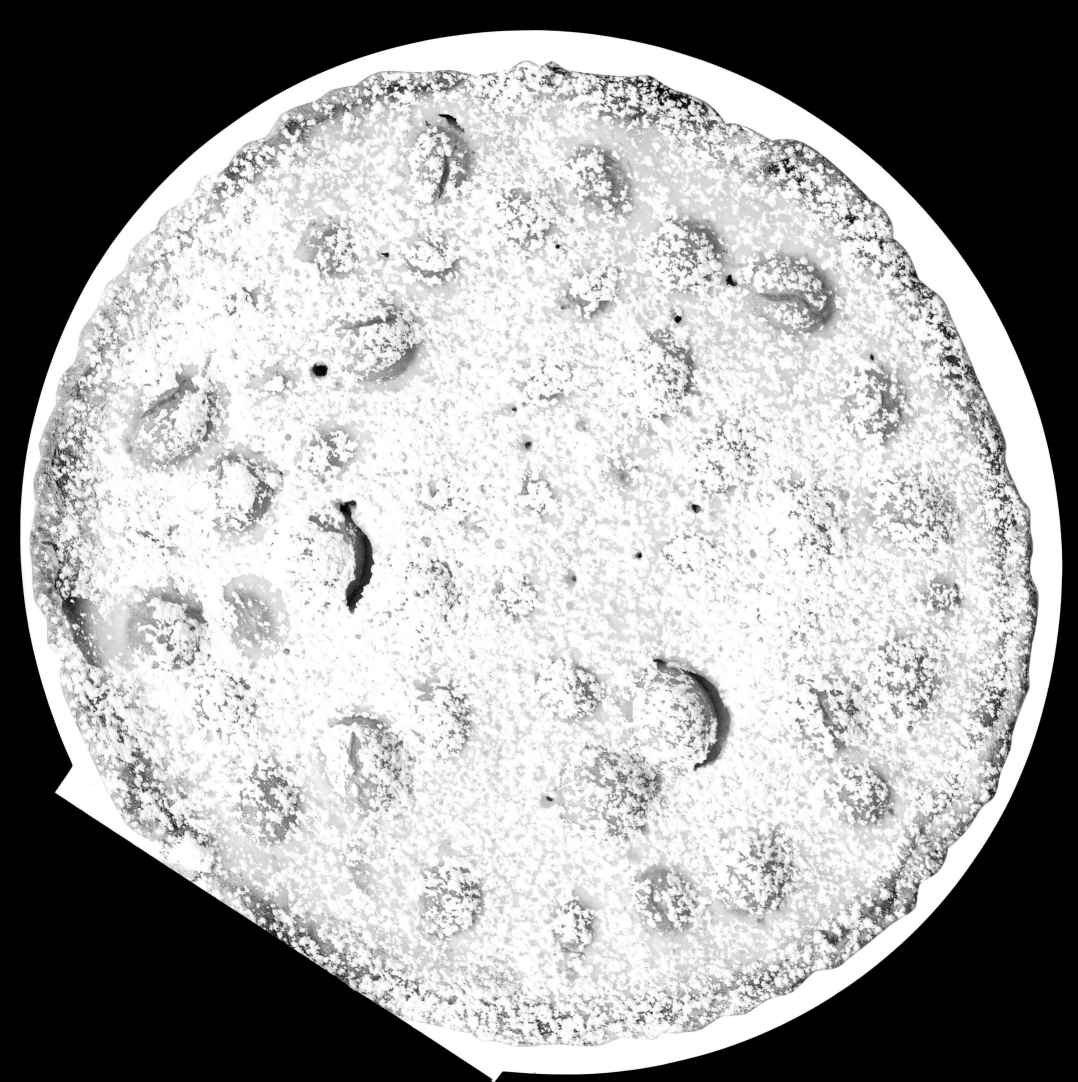

banoffee pie

CRUST
Sweet tart pastry (see pages 8–9)

FILLING
1 (14-ounce/400-g) can sweetened condensed milk · 1/3 cup (70 g) firmly packed dark brown sugar · 3 large bananas · 1 cup (250 ml) heavy (double) cream · 2 tablespoons confectioners' (icing) sugar

SERVES 8 · PREPARATION 30 MINUTES + 1 HOUR 30 MINUTES TO CHILL & COOL
COOKING 30–40 MINUTES

Banoffee pie is an English dessert made from bananas, cream, and boiled condensed milk. Its name is a combination of banana and toffee.

CRUST **1. Prepare** the sweet tart pastry and chill for at least 30 minutes. **2. Line** an 11-inch (28-cm) tart pan with a removable bottom with the pastry and bake blind following the instructions on page 9. Let cool a little while you prepare the filling. FILLING **3. Combine** the condensed milk and brown sugar in a small saucepan over medium-low heat and simmer, stirring constantly, until it becomes a thick caramel sauce, about 20 minutes. Remove from the heat, allow to cool a little, then refrigerate until chilled, about 1 hour. **4. Pour** the chilled caramel sauce into the baked pastry crust. **5. Peel** and slice the bananas. Arrange on top of the filling. **6. Beat** the cream and confectioners' sugar until thickened. Spoon the whipped cream onto the center of the pie, half covering the banana layer. **7. Serve** at once.

• If you liked this recipe, try the fruit tart on page 26.

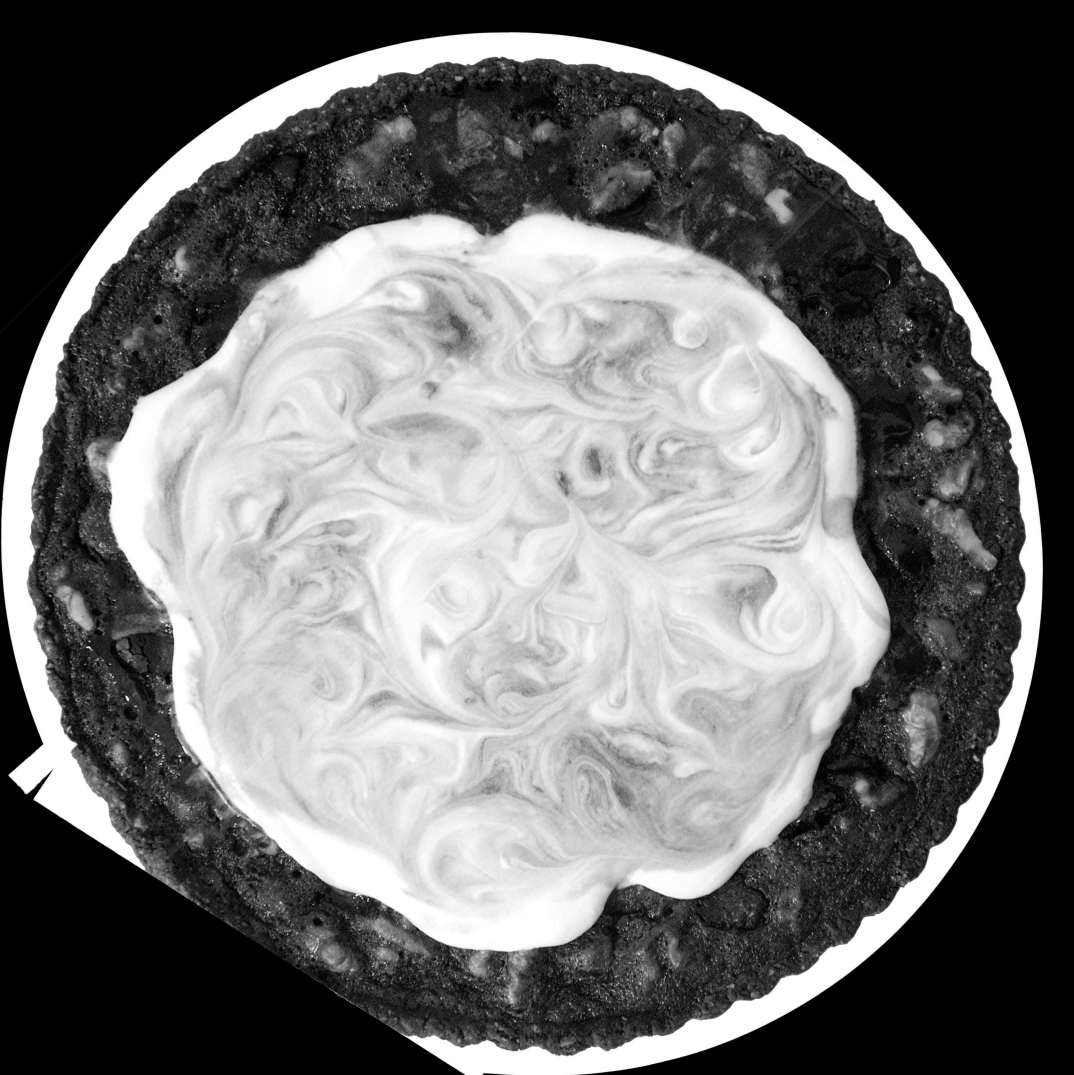

CRUST

Chocolate sweet tart pastry (see pages 8–9)

WHITE CHOCOLATE FILLING

2¹/₂ cups (600 ml) heavy (double) cream · 12 ounces (350 g) white chocolate, coarsely chopped · 4 limes, peeled and very thinly sliced, to decorate

SERVES 8 · **PREPARATION** 45 MINUTES + 2 HOURS 30 MINUTES TO CHILL
COOKING 15–20 MINUTES

white chocolate
lime pie

68

CRUST **1. Prepare** the chocolate sweet tart pastry and chill for at least 30 minutes. **2. Line** an 11-inch (28-cm) tart pan with a removable bottom with the pastry and bake blind following the instructions on page 9. Let cool a little while you prepare the filling.

FILLING **3. Heat** the cream in a medium saucepan until it just comes to a boil. Put the white chocolate in a large bowl and pour the hot cream over the top. Stir until the chocolate is melted and the mixture is well blended. Place a sheet of plastic wrap (cling film) on the surface and chill in the refrigerator for at least 2 hours. **4. Spoon** the filling into the cooled baked pastry shell. Decorate with the sliced limes. **5. Chill** in the refrigerator until ready to serve.

If you liked this recipe, try the orange ricotta tart on page 24.

pear & frangipane tart

CRUST

Sweet tart pastry (see pages 8–9)

FILLING

⅓ cup (90 g) butter, softened · ½ cup (100 g) firmly packed light brown sugar
½ teaspoon almond extract (essence) · 2 large eggs · 1 cup (100 g) ground almonds
2 tablespoons cornstarch (cornflour) · 4–5 tablespoons greengage or yellow plum preserves
3 firm ripe pears · 2 tablespoons clear apple jelly · 1 teaspoon freshly squeezed lemon juice

SERVES 8 · **PREPARATION** 45 MINUTES + 30 MINUTES TO CHILL · **COOKING** 45–55 MINUTES

CRUST **1. Prepare** the sweet tart pastry and chill for at least 30 minutes. **2. Line** an 11-inch (28-cm) tart pan with a removable bottom with the pastry and bake blind following the instructions on page 9. Let cool a little while you prepare the filling.

FILLING **3. Preheat** the oven to 350°F (180°C/gas 4). **4. Combine** the butter, brown sugar, and almond extract in a medium bowl. Beat with an electric mixer at medium speed until smooth and creamy. Add the eggs one at a time, beating until just combined after each addition. Beat in the ground almonds and cornstarch. **5. Spread** the preserves over the bottom of the baked tart crust and pour in the almond mixture. Smooth the surface with a palette knife. **6. Peel,** halve, and core the pears. Place each half cut-side down on a cutting board. Slice thinly lengthwise. Arrange in a fan shape on top of the filling. **7. Bake** for 35–40 minutes, until the filling is set and golden. **8. Heat** the apple jelly and lemon juice in a small saucepan over low heat until bubbling, 1–2 minutes. Spread over the tart. **9. Serve** warm.

You can vary this tart by replacing the pears with 4 large, firm-fleshed peaches. Peel and pit the peaches, then slice thinly and place on the frangipane as you would with the pears.

• **If you liked this recipe, try the pear & almond tart on page 18.**

raspberry & frangipane tart

CRUST
Sweet tart pastry (see pages 8–9)

FRANGIPANE FILLING
½ cup (100 g) superfine (caster) sugar • ⅓ cup (90 g) unsalted butter, softened • ⅓ cup (50 g) all-purpose (plain) flour • 1½ cups (150 g) ground almonds
2 large eggs • 1 teaspoon vanilla extract (essence)
1 cup (150 g) fresh raspberries

SERVES 8 • PREPARATION 30 MINUTES + 1 HOUR TO CHILL • COOKING 45–55 MINUTES

CRUST **1. Prepare** the sweet tart pastry and chill for at least 30 minutes. **2. Line** an 11-inch (28-cm) tart pan with a removable bottom with the pastry and bake blind following the instructions on page 9. Let cool a little while you prepare the filling.

FILLING **3. Preheat** the oven to 325°F (170°C/gas 3). **4. Pulse** the sugar, butter, flour, ground almonds, and vanilla in a food processor on medium speed until a smooth paste is formed, about 2 minutes. 5. **Spoon** the frangipane mixture into the tart shell and smooth using a spatula or the back of the spoon. Press the raspberries decoratively into the top of the tart. **6. Bake** for 35–40 minutes, until the frangipane is golden brown. **7. Let cool** to room temperature before serving.

• If you liked this recipe, try the pear & frangipane tart on page 70.

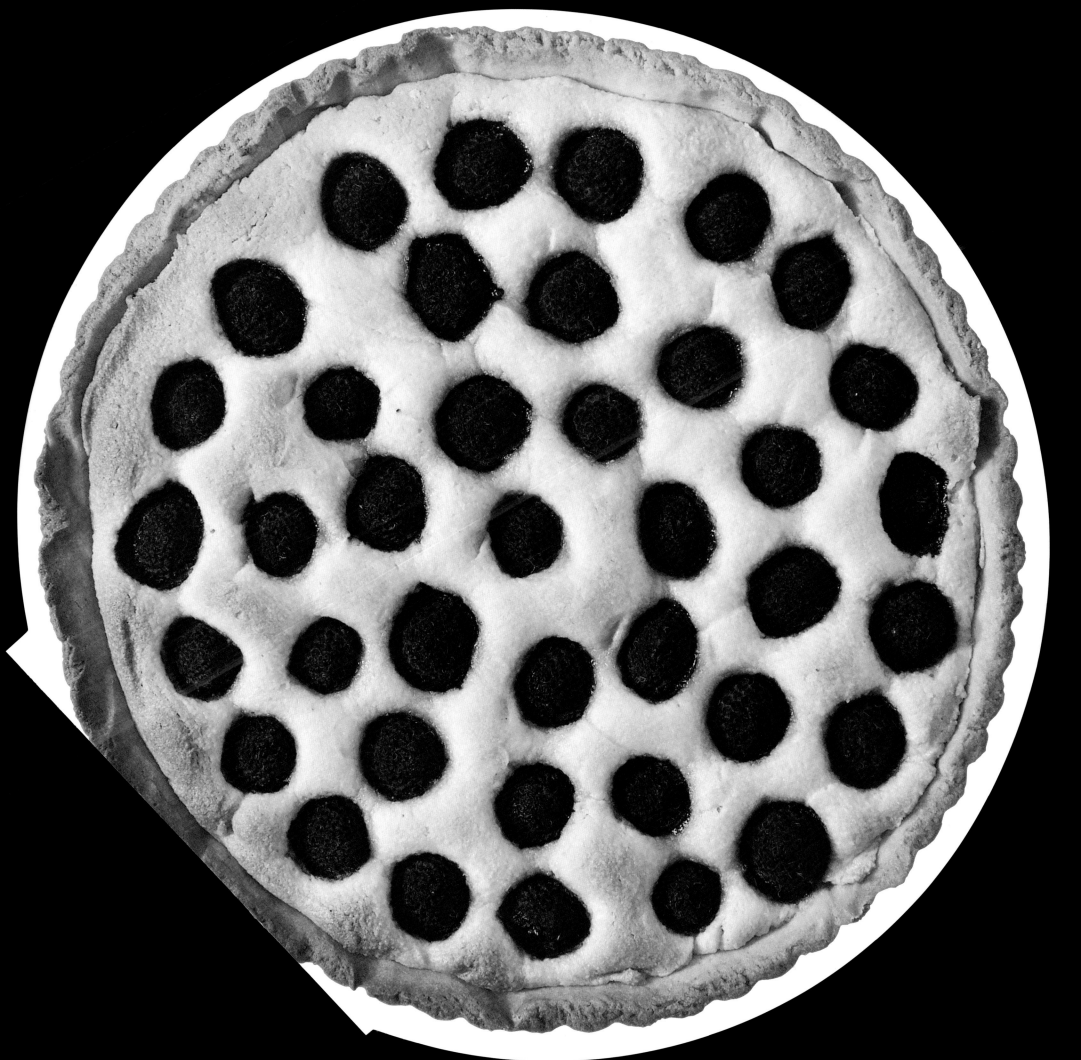

divine mousse pie

SERVES 8 . PREPARATION 30 MINUTES + 6 HOURS TO CHILL & COOL . COOKING 15–20 MINUTES

CRUST

Chocolate sweet tart pastry (see pages 8–9)

CHOCOLATE MOUSSE FILLING

1 pound (500 g) dark chocolate · ½ cup (125 ml) milk · 6 large eggs, separated
½ cup (75 g) confectioners' (icing) sugar · ¾ cup (180 ml) heavy (double) cream
¼ teaspoon cream of tartar · 2 tablespoons granulated sugar

TOPPING

1 cup (250 ml) heavy (double) cream · 2 tablespoons unsweetened cocoa powder · 2 tablespoons
confectioners' (icing) sugar · 1 teaspoon amaretto or other almond liqueur

CRUST 1. Prepare the chocolate sweet tart pastry and chill for at least 30 minutes. **2. Line** an 11-inch (28-cm) tart pan with a removable bottom with the pastry and bake blind, following the instructions on page 9. Let cool. **FILLING 3. Melt** the chocolate with the milk in a double boiler over barely simmering water. **4. Beat** the egg yolks and confectioners' sugar in a double boiler until well blended. Stir in the chocolate mixture. Simmer over barely simmering water, stirring constantly with a wooden spoon, until the mixture lightly coats a metal spoon or registers 160°F (71°C) on an instant-read thermometer. Plunge the pan into a bowl of ice water and stir until the mixture has cooled. **5. Beat** the cream in a large bowl with an electric mixer at high speed until stiff. Fold into the chocolate mixture. **6. Beat** the egg whites, cream of tartar, and granulated sugar with the mixer at medium speed until stiff peaks form. Fold into the chocolate mixture. **7. Spoon** the mousse into the baked pastry crust. Refrigerate until set, at least 1 hour. **TOPPING 8. Beat** the cream, cocoa, confectioners' sugar, and amaretto in a large bowl with an electric mixer at high speed until stiff. **9. Spoon** the cream into a pastry bag fitted with a ¾-inch (2-cm) star tip. Decorate the top of the pie with a border of cream.

• **If you liked this recipe, try the strawberry mousse tart on page 20.**

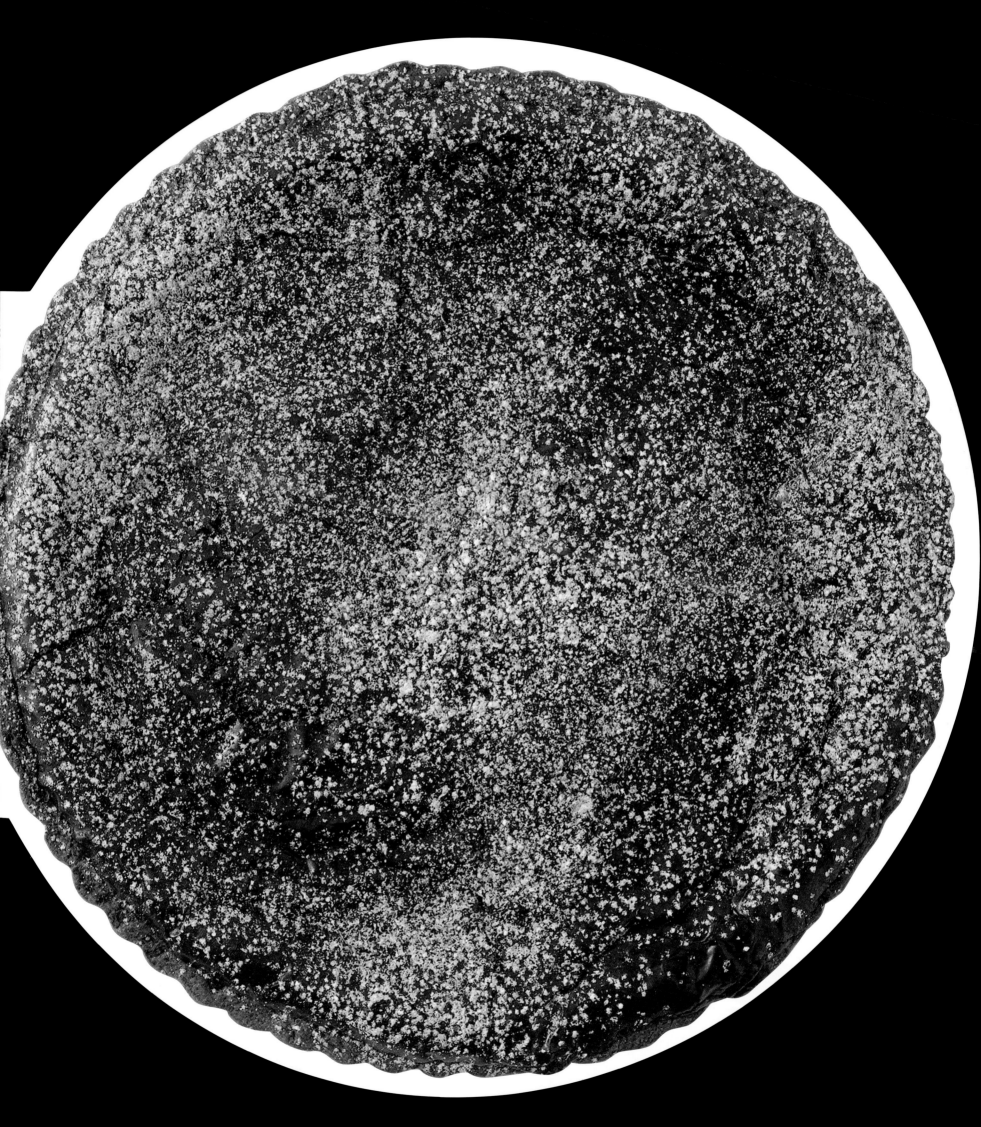

CRUST

Chocolate sweet tart pastry (see pages 8–9)

FILLING & TOPPING

7 ounces (200 g) dark chocolate, chopped • $^1/_3$ cup (90 ml) heavy (double) cream
1 teaspoon vanilla extract (essence) • $^1/_3$ cup (90 g) unsalted butter, softened
1$^1/_4$ cups (250 g) sugar • 4 large eggs, separated + 1 large egg yolk
1 cup (100 g) ground almonds

SERVES 8 • **PREPARATION** 45 MINUTES + 1 HOUR TO CHILL & COOL • **COOKING** 35–45 MINUTES

chocolate meringue
pie

78

CRUST **1. Prepare** the chocolate sweet tart pastry and chill for at least 30 minutes. **2. Line** an 11-inch (28-cm) tart pan with a removable bottom with the pastry and bake blind, following the instructions on page 9. Let cool a little while you prepare the filling.

FILLING **3. Preheat** the oven to 350°F (180°C/gas 4). **4. Combine** the chocolate, cream, and vanilla in a double boiler over barely simmering water and stir until smooth. Set aside to cool. **5. Beat** the butter and $^1/_2$ cup (100 g) of sugar in a small bowl with an electric mixer on high speed until pale and creamy. Add the egg yolks and chocolate mixture, beating to combine. Fold in the ground almonds. **6. Spoon** the filling into the baked tart crust. **7. Bake** for 10 minutes. **8. While the filling** is baking, beat the egg whites in a medium bowl with an electric mixer on medium speed until foamy. Gradually add the remaining $^3/_4$ cup (150 g) sugar, whisking until smooth, glossy peaks form. **9. Spoon** the meringue over the filling and bake for 15–20 minutes, until golden. **10. Serve** warm or at room temperature.

Serve this amazing pie on birthdays, anniversaries, and other special occasions.

● If you liked this recipe, try the red currant meringue pie on page 118.

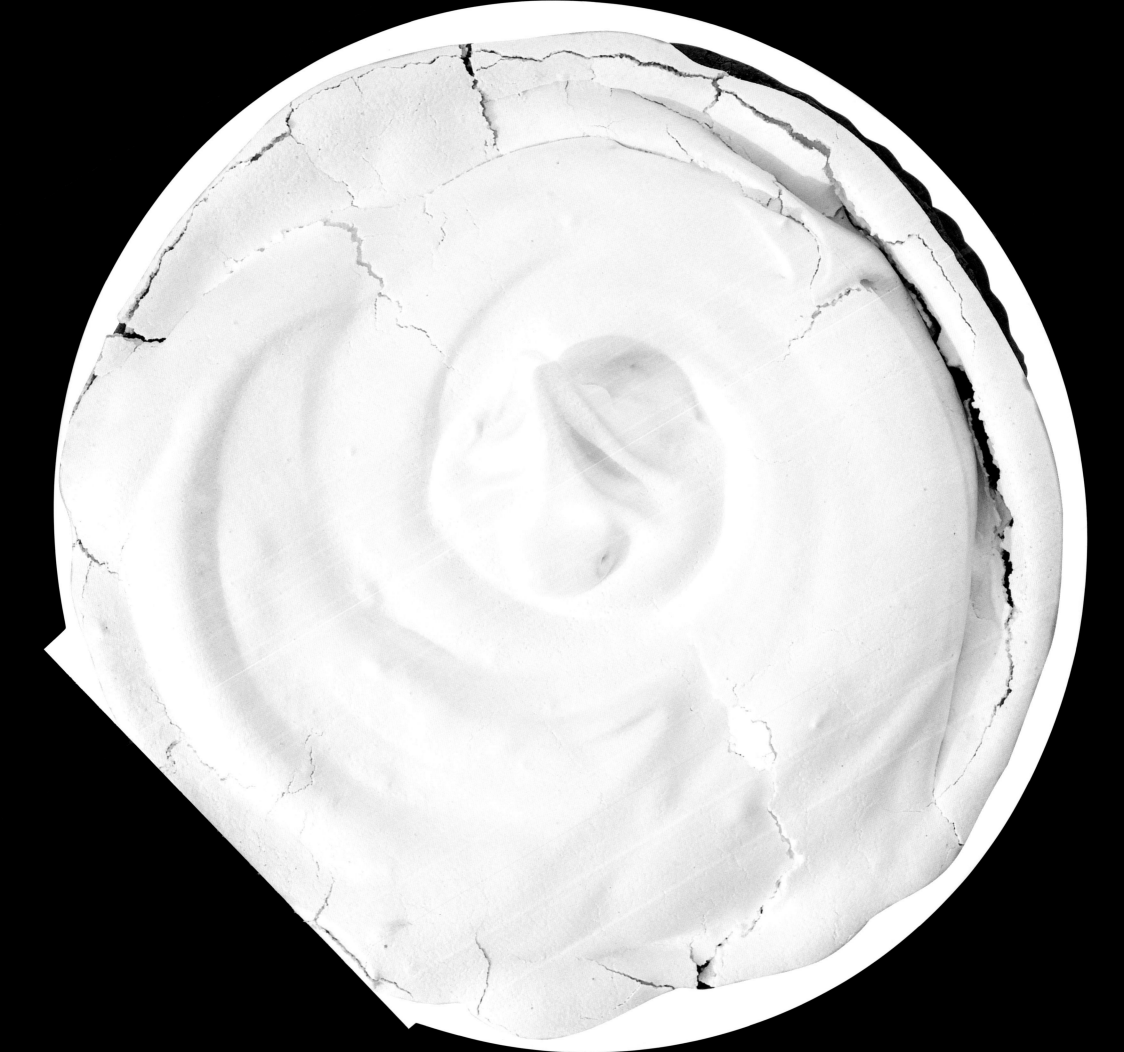

cool chocolate macadamia tart

CRUST

3 cups (300 g) graham cracker or digestive biscuit crumbs • 3/4 cup (180 g) salted butter, melted

FILLING

10 ounces (300 g) dark chocolate, coarsely chopped • 1½ cups (375 g) cream cheese, softened • 3/4 cup (150 g) sugar • 2 teaspoons vanilla extract (essence) • 1 cup (120 g) macadamia nuts, coarsely chopped • 2½ cups (600 ml) heavy (double) cream

SERVES 8 • **PREPARATION** 45 MINUTES + 4–6 HOURS TO FREEZE • **COOKING** 5 MINUTES

CRUST **1. Lightly butter** an 11-inch (28-cm) tart pan with a removable bottom. **2. Combine** the crumbs and butter in a bowl and mix well. Firmly press the mixture into the bottom and sides of the pan. FILLING **3. Melt** the chocolate in a double boiler over barely simmering water. Remove from the heat and let cool a little. **4. Beat** the chocolate, cream cheese, sugar, and vanilla in a large bowl with an electric mixer at medium speed until smooth. Stir in the macadamia

nuts. **5. Beat** the cream with an electric mixer on medium-high speed until thickened. Use a large spatula to fold about one-fourth of the cream into the chocolate mixture. Fold in the remaining whipped cream. **6. Spoon** the filling into the crust. Cover with foil and freeze for 4–6 hours. **7. To serve,** carefully loosen and remove the sides of the pan. Let stand at room temperature for 5 minutes before serving.

Chocolate lovers will adore this tart with its rich, creamy filling. You can also serve it with fresh berries and whipped cream.

• **If you liked this recipe,** try the chocolate almond cream pie on page 122.

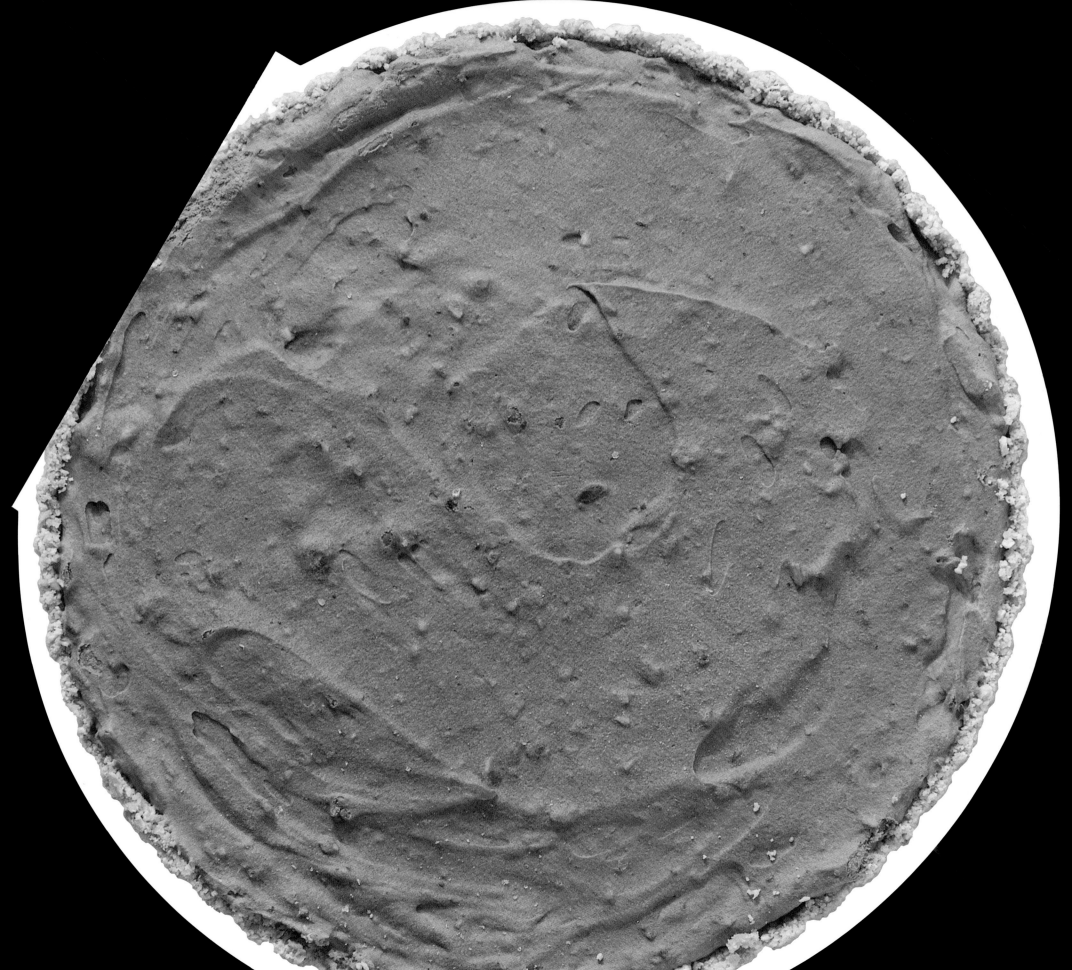

rich mocha pie

CRUST

3 cups (300 g) plain chocolate cookie (biscuit) crumbs · 1½ tablespoons instant coffee granules · ½ cup (100 g) sugar · ½ cup (125 g) butter, melted

FILLING

8 ounces (250 g) dark chocolate, coarsely chopped · 1 tablespoon instant coffee granules · ½ cup (125 ml) cold water · 1 tablespoon unflavored gelatin · 6 large eggs, separated · ¾ cup (150 g) sugar · 1 cup (250 ml) heavy (double) cream · Milk chocolate curls, to decorate

SERVES 8 · **PREPARATION** 30 MINUTES + 7 HOURS TO CHILL · **COOKING** 30 MINUTES

CRUST **1. Preheat** the oven to 350°F (180°C/gas 4). Butter an 11-inch (28-cm) pie pan. **2. Combine** the cookie crumbs, coffee, and sugar in a large bowl. Stir in the butter and mix well. Press the crust into the bottom and along the sides of the prepared pan. **3. Bake** for 10 minutes. Cool on a rack.

FILLING **4. Melt** the chocolate in a double boiler over barely simmering water. Remove from the heat and stir in the coffee. Set aside to cool. **5. Put** the cold water in a small bowl. Sprinkle with the gelatin and set aside to soften. **6. Combine** the egg yolks and half the sugar in a double boiler over barely simmering water. Stir with a wooden spoon until the sugar is dissolved and the mixture coats the spoon. **7. Add** the gelatin mixture and stir until the gelatin is dissolved. **8. Remove** from the heat and stir in the melted chocolate. Let cool to room temperature, then chill in the refrigerator for 1 hour. **9. Chill** the chocolate mixture and then beat the cream with 2 tablespoons of the remaining sugar until stiff peaks form. Fold into the chocolate mixture. **10. Beat** the egg whites and remaining sugar with an electric mixer at medium speed until stiff peaks form. Gently fold into the chocolate mixture. **11. Spoon** the filling into the pie crust and chill in the refrigerator for at least 6 hours before serving. **12. Top** with the milk chocolate curls just before serving.

Our word "mocha" comes from a seaport in Yemen that shipped choice coffee all over the world. Nowadays it also means a dish flavored with a mixture of chocolate and coffee.

● **If you liked this recipe,** try the divine mousse pie on page 74.

chocolate Linzer torte

CRUST

1²/3 cups (250 g) all-purpose (plain) flour
1 cup (150 g) finely ground almonds · 3/4 cup (150 g) sugar
1/3 cup (50 g) unsweetened cocoa powder · 1 cup (250 g) salted butter
2 large egg yolks · 1 teaspoon vanilla extract (essence)

FILLING

1 cup (180 g) chopped dried apricots · 1/3 cup (90 ml) freshly squeezed orange juice
1/4 cup (60 ml) apricot liqueur · 2 cups (500 g) apricot preserves (jam)

SERVES 8 · **PREPARATION** 45 MINUTES · **COOKING** 45–55 MINUTES

CRUST **1. Preheat** the oven to 350°F (180°C/gas 4). **2. Combine** the flour, ground almonds, sugar, and cocoa in a food processor and pulse until well mixed. **3. Add** the butter and process until crumbly. **4. Add** the egg yolks and vanilla and pulse until the dough begins to hold together. **5. Remove** one-third of the dough. Wrap in plastic wrap (cling film) and chill in the refrigerator. **6. Press** the remaining two-thirds of the dough into the bottom and sides of an 11-inch (28-cm) tart pan with a removable bottom. **7. Bake** for 15 minutes, until firm. Let cool in the pan on a wire rack. FILLING **8. Heat** the apricots and orange juice in a small saucepan over medium heat, stirring occasionally. Bring to a boil and simmer over very low heat for 10 minutes. **9. Remove** from the heat and stir in the apricot liqueur and 1²/3 cups (400 g) of the apricot preserves (reserve the rest to glaze). Mix until smooth then let cool and thicken slightly before spreading over the bottom of the cooled pastry crust. **10. Roll out** the remaining dough on a floured work surface to about 1/4 inch (5 mm) thick. Cut into 1/2-inch (1-cm) wide strips, and use them to create a lattice pattern on top of the pie (see page 11). **11. Bake** for 30–35 minutes, until the filling is bubbly. **12. Let cool** on a wire rack, then carefully remove from the pan. **13. Bring** the remaining apricot preserves to a boil in a small pan over low heat. Using a pastry brush, evenly brush the top of the tart with the preserves. **14. Serve** warm or at room temperature.

This famous pie comes from the town of Linz, in Austria. You can also omit the dried apricots and replace the apricot preserves (jam) with the same quantity of raspberry preserves.

● **If you liked this recipe, try the Neapolitan pie on page 124.**

FREE-FORM CRUST

2 cups (300 g) all-purpose (plain) flour
3 tablespoons superfine (caster) sugar • 2/3 cup (180 g)
salted butter, chilled and cubed • 3 tablespoons iced water

FILLING

1 cup (200 g) gooseberries or raspberries • 2 cups (300 g) blackberries or blueberries
4 big red or yellow plums (about 10 ounces/300 g), pitted and quartered
1/2 cup (100 g) granulated sugar • 1 tablespoon cornstarch (cornflour) • 1 large egg, separated
1 tablespoon ground almonds or semolina • 1 tablespoon milk • 2 tablespoons raw sugar, to sprinkle

SERVES 4 • PREPARATION 30 MINUTES + 30 MINUTES TO CHILL • COOKING 25–35 MINUTES

merry berry pie

CRUST **1. Mix** the flour and superfine sugar in a large bowl. Cut in the butter with a pastry blender until the mixture resembles coarse crumbs. **2. Stir in** the water to form a smooth dough. Bring together with both hands and knead lightly. It may need a little more water if crumbly, or flour if sticky. Shape into a ball and wrap in plastic wrap (cling film). Refrigerate for 30 minutes. FILLING **3. Toss** the berries and plums with the sugar and cornstarch in a bowl. **4. Preheat** the oven to 400°F (200°C/gas 6). Butter an 11-inch (28-cm) tart pan. **5. Dust** a work surface with flour and roll out the pastry into a sheet about 1/4 inch (5 mm) thick and 20 inches (50 cm) in diameter. **6. Roll loosely** over the rolling pin and place in the pan, leaving the edges overhanging. Brush with a little egg white and sprinkle with the ground almonds or semolina to keep it from becoming soggy. **7. Spoon** the berry mixture onto the center of the pastry. Pull up the edges of the pastry as far as they will go, partially enclosing the filling and pinching the corners to seal. **8. Whisk** the egg yolk and milk in a small bowl and brush over the pie. Sprinkle with the raw sugar. **9. Bake** for 25–35 minutes, or until the pastry is golden brown and the juices from the fruit are bubbling. **10. Serve** hot.

Serve this hearty fruit tart with fresh cream or custard.

● If you liked this recipe, try the free-form apricot pie on page 114.

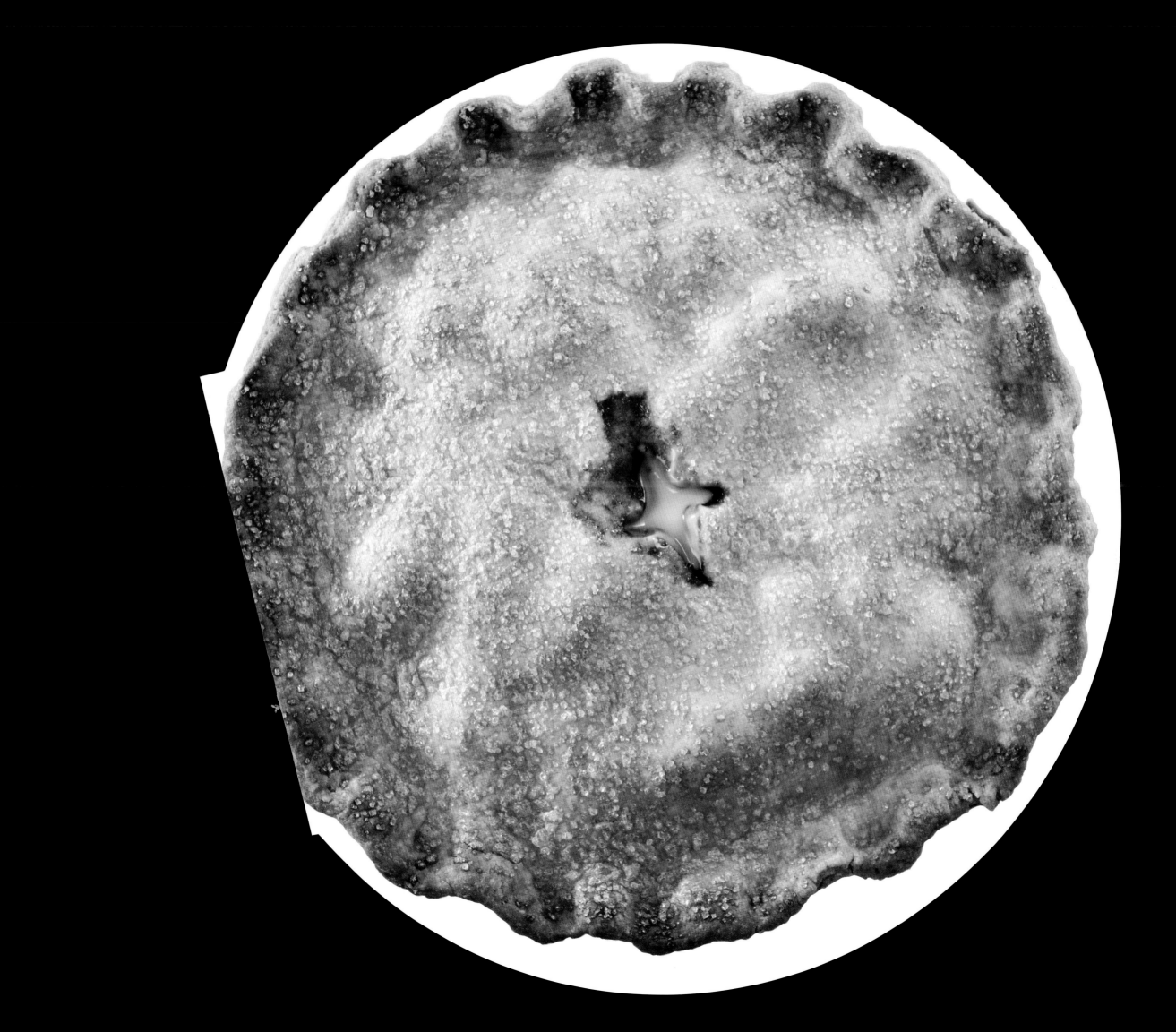

CRUST

Pie crust pastry (see pages 10–11)

BLUEBERRY FILLING

4 cups (600 g) fresh or frozen blueberries • ¹/3 cup (30 g) ground almonds
¹/3 cup (75 g) granulated sugar • 2 teaspoons finely grated lemon zest
Milk, to glaze • Raw sugar, to sprinkle

SERVES 8 • **PREPARATION** 30 MINUTES + 1 HOUR 30 MINUTES TO CHILL
COOKING 30-40 MINUTES

blueberry pie

CRUST **1. Prepare** the pie crust pastry. Divide into two equal portions. Wrap both in plastic wrap (cling film) and refrigerate for 1 hour. **2. Roll out** one piece of pastry following the instructions on page 11 and use it to line a 10-inch (28-cm) pie pan. Refrigerate for 1 hour.
FILLING **3. Preheat** the oven to 400°F (200°C/gas 6). **4. Combine** the blueberries, almonds, granulated sugar, and lemon zest in a medium bowl, mixing well. **5. Spoon** the filling into the prepared pan. **6. Roll out** the remaining piece of pastry into a circle about 11 inches (28 cm) in diameter. Place over the filling, tucking the overhang under the bottom crust pastry. Crimp or flute the edges. Make a hole in the top with a sharp knife. Brush with milk and sprinkle with raw sugar. **7. Bake** for 30-40 minutes, or until the pastry is golden brown. **8. Serve** warm.

Replace the blueberries with blackberries or boysenberries for an equally delicious pie.

● If you liked this recipe, try the blackberry custard pie on page 90.

apple & strawberry pie

SERVES 8 • **PREPARATION** 30 MINUTES + 1 HOUR 30 MINUTES TO CHILL • **COOKING** 45–55 MINUTES

CRUST

Pie crust pastry (see pages 10–11)

APPLE & STRAWBERRY FILLING

$1\frac{1}{2}$ pounds (750 g) tart apples, such as Granny Smiths • 2–3 tablespoons water • 3 cups (450 g) fresh or frozen strawberries, halved • $\frac{1}{2}$ cup (100 g) firmly packed light brown sugar • 1 tablespoon cornstarch (cornflour) 1 teaspoon finely grated orange zest • 1 teaspoon ground cinnamon • 3 tablespoons milk, to glaze • Raw sugar, to sprinkle

CRUST **1. Prepare** the pie crust pastry. Divide into two equal portions. Wrap both in plastic wrap (cling film) and refrigerate for 1 hour. **2. Roll out** one piece of pastry following the instructions on page 11 and use it to line a 10-inch (28-cm) pie pan. Refrigerate for 30 minutes.

FILLING **3. Preheat** the oven to 400°F (200°C/gas 6). **4. Peel,** core, and thinly slice the apples. Cook in a large saucepan with the water over medium heat for 5 minutes. Add the strawberries, brown sugar, cornstarch, orange zest, and cinnamon and simmer until the apples begin to soften, about 10 minutes. **5. Remove** from the heat and pour the filling into the prepared pie crust. **6. Roll out** the remaining piece of pastry into a circle about 11 inches (28 cm) in diameter. Place over the filling, tucking the overhang under the bottom crust pastry. Crimp or flute the edges. Make a hole in the top with a sharp knife. Brush with milk and sprinkle with raw sugar. **7. Bake** for 30–40 minutes, until the pastry is golden brown. **8. Serve** warm.

• **If you liked this recipe, try the apple pie on page 106.**

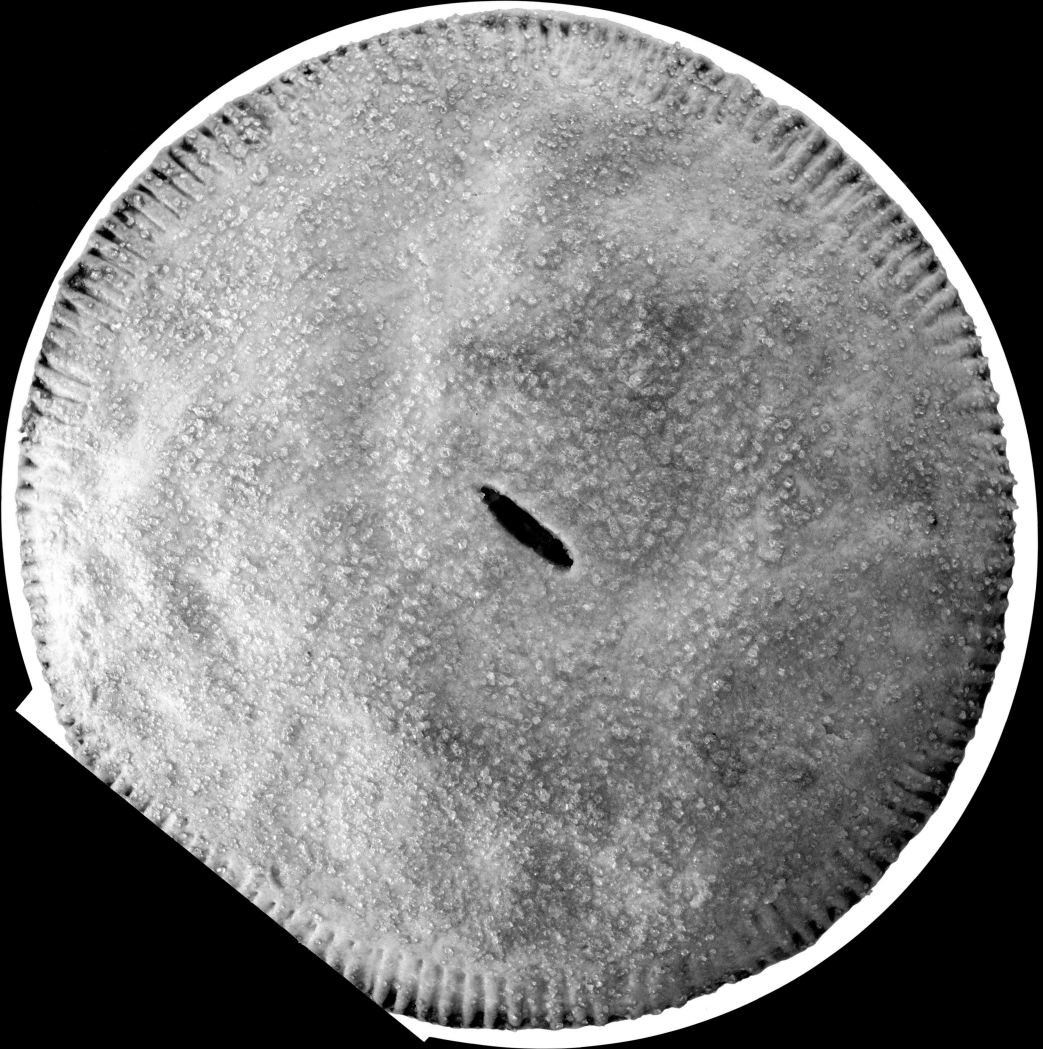

CRUST

Pie crust pastry (see pages 10–11)

PEACH FILLING

¹/₂ cup (100 g) granulated sugar • 2 tablespoons all-purpose (plain) flour
2 tablespoons ground almonds • 1 teaspoon ground cinnamon • 2 pounds (1 kg)
peaches, peeled, pitted, and sliced • 1 tablespoon freshly squeezed lemon juice
1 tablespoon unsalted butter • 1 large egg, lightly beaten • Raw sugar, to sprinkle
Whipped cream or crème fraîche, to serve

SERVES 8 • **PREPARATION** 40 MINUTES + 1 HOUR 30 MINUTES TO CHILL • **COOKING** 30–40 MINUTES

peach pie

98

CRUST **1. Prepare** the pie crust pastry. Divide into two equal portions. Wrap both in plastic wrap (cling film) and refrigerate for 1 hour. **2. Roll out** one piece of pastry following the instructions on page 11 and use it to line a 10-inch (28-cm) pie pan. Refrigerate for 1 hour.
FILLING **3. Preheat** the oven to 400°F (200°C/gas 6). **4. Combine** the granulated sugar, flour, almonds, and cinnamon in a medium bowl. Add the peaches, pour in the lemon juice, and toss to coat. **5. Spoon** the filling into the prepared pie crust and dot with butter. **6. Roll out** the remaining piece of pastry into a circle about 11 inches (28 cm) in diameter. Place over the filling, tucking the overhang under the bottom crust pastry. Crimp or flute the edges. Make a hole in the top with a sharp knife. Brush with the egg and sprinkle with raw sugar. **7. Bake** for 30–40 minutes, until the pastry is golden brown. **8. Serve** warm with a dollop of whipped cream or crème fraîche.

If fresh peaches are out of season, use the same quantity of well-drained unsweetened canned peaches.

● If you liked this recipe, try the rhubarb lattice pie on page 112.

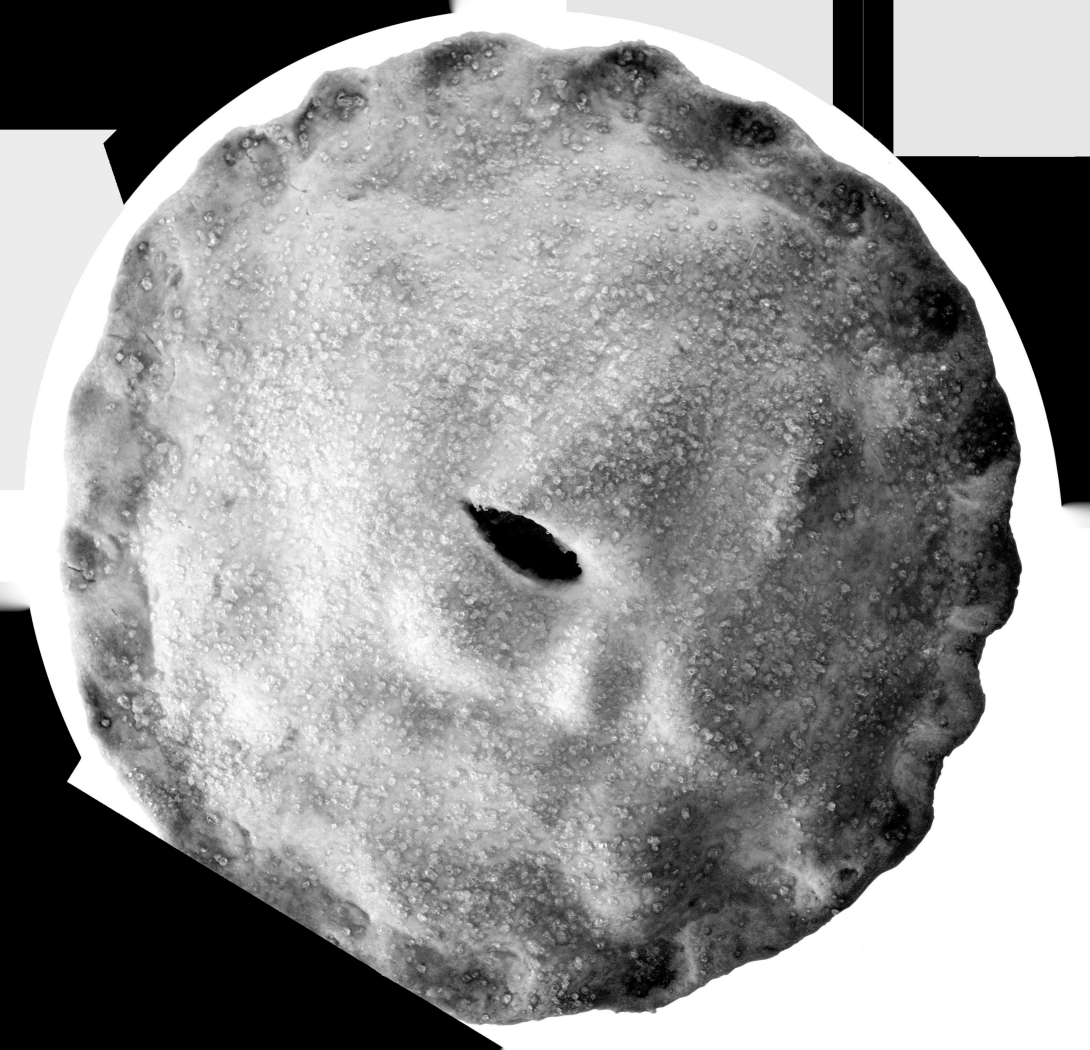

fruits of the forest pie

CRUST
Pie crust pastry (see pages 10–11)

BERRY FILLING
2 cups (300 g) fresh or frozen blueberries · 2 cups (300 g) fresh or frozen blackberries · 2 cups (300 g) fresh or frozen raspberries · 1/2 cup (100 g) granulated sugar · 3 tablespoons all-purpose (plain) flour · 1 teaspoon ground cinnamon · 1/2 teaspoon ground nutmeg · 2 teaspoons finely grated lemon zest · 1 large egg, lightly beaten · Raw sugar, to sprinkle

SERVES 8 · PREPARATION 30 MINUTES + 1 HOUR 30 MINUTES TO CHILL · COOKING 30–40 MINUTES

CRUST **1. Prepare** the pie crust pastry. Divide into two equal portions. Wrap both in plastic wrap (cling film) and refrigerate for 1 hour. **2. Roll out** one piece of pastry following the instructions on page 11 and use it to line a 10-inch (28-cm) pie pan. Reserve any scraps and add to the dough remaining in the refrigerator. Refrigerate for 1 hour.

FILLING **3. Preheat** the oven to 400°F (200°C/gas 6). **4. Combine** the blueberries, blackberries, raspberries, sugar, flour, cinnamon, nutmeg, and lemon zest in a medium bowl, stirring to combine. **5. Spoon** the filling into the prepared pie crust. **6. Roll out** the remaining piece of pastry and cut into a circle about 11 inches in diameter. Place over the filling, tucking the overhang under the bottom crust pastry. Crimp or flute the edges. Gather the scraps, reroll, and cut into decorative shapes.

Moisten with water and stick onto the top crust. Make a few slits in the top crust. Brush with beaten egg and sprinkle with raw sugar. **7. Bake** for 30–40 minutes, or until the pastry is golden brown. **8. Serve** warm.

You can use any combination of berries for this pie as long as the total amounts are the same.

● **If you liked this recipe, try the blueberry pie on page 92.**

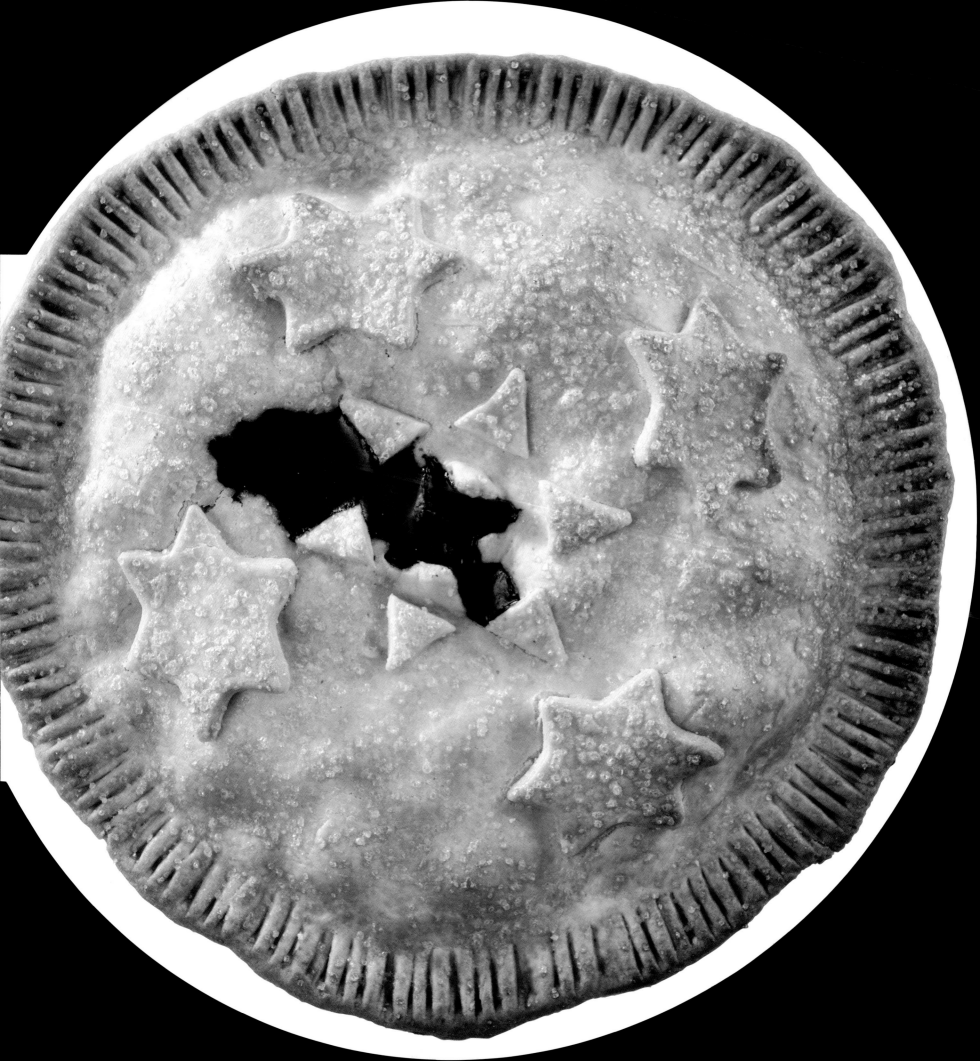

black plum pie

CRUST

Pie crust pastry (see pages 10–11)

PLUM FILLING

1/2 cup (100 g) firmly packed dark brown sugar · 4 tablespoons all-purpose (plain) flour · 1 teaspoon ground cinnamon · 2 pounds (1 kg) black plums, peeled, pitted, and sliced · 1 tablespoon freshly squeezed lemon juice 1 tablespoon unsalted butter · 1 large egg, lightly beaten · Raw sugar, to sprinkle

SERVES 6–8 · **PREPARATION** 40 MINUTES + 1 HOUR 30 MINUTES TO CHILL · **COOKING** 30–40 MINUTES

CRUST **1. Prepare** the pie crust pastry. Divide into two portions, one slightly larger than the other. Wrap both in plastic wrap (cling film) and refrigerate for 1 hour. **2. Roll out** one piece of pastry following the instructions on page 11 and use it to line a 10-inch (28-cm) pie pan. Refrigerate for 1 hour. FILLING **3. Preheat** the oven to 400°F (200°C/gas 6). **4. Combine** the brown sugar, flour, and cinnamon in a medium bowl. Add the plums and lemon juice, stirring to coat. **5. Spoon** the filling into the prepared pie crust and dot with butter. **6. Roll out** the remaining piece of pastry. Following the instructions on page 11, cut into strips and lay on top of the filling in a lattice pattern. Press down with your fingers around the edges to seal. Cut off any excess pastry and brush with the beaten egg. Sprinkle with the raw sugar. **7. Bake** for 30–40 minutes, or until the pastry is golden brown. **8. Serve** warm.

● If you liked this recipe, try the ricotta & plum tart on page 46.

102

apple pie

CRUST

Pie crust pastry (see pages 10–11)

FILLING

2 pounds (1 kg) tart cooking apples, such as Granny Smiths · 3/4 cup (150 g) granulated sugar · 1 1/2 tablespoons freshly squeezed orange or lemon juice 3 tablespoons all-purpose (plain) flour · 1 teaspoon ground cinnamon · 3 tablespoons milk, to glaze · Raw sugar, to sprinkle

SERVES 8 · **PREPARATION** 30 MINUTES + 1 HOUR 30 MINUTES TO CHILL · **COOKING** 35–45 MINUTES

CRUST **1. Prepare** the pie crust pastry. Divide into two equal portions. Wrap both in plastic wrap (cling film) and refrigerate for 1 hour. **2. Roll out** one piece of pastry following the instructions on page 11 and use it to line a 10-inch (28-cm) pie pan. Refrigerate for 1 hour. FILLING **3. Preheat** the oven to 400°F (200°C/gas 6). **4. Peel,** core, and slice the apples. Mix them with the sugar, orange juice, flour, and cinnamon. **5. Spoon** the filling into the prepared pie crust. **6. Roll** out the remaining piece of pastry and use it as a lid to cover the filling, pressing down with your fingers around the edges to seal. Cut off any excess pastry. Make two holes in the center of the pie lid to allow steam to escape during baking. Brush with the milk and sprinkle with the raw sugar. **7. Bake** for 10 minutes. Decrease the oven temperature to 375°F (190°C/gas 5) and bake for 25–30 minutes, until the pastry is golden. **8. Serve** warm or at room temperature.

If you liked this recipe, try the apple & strawberry pie on page 96.

raspberry & coconut pie

SERVES 8 • **PREPARATION** 45 MINUTES + 1 HOUR TO CHILL • **COOKING** 35–40 MINUTES

CRUST

2 1/2 cups (375 g) all-purpose (plain) flour • 1 cup (150 g) confectioners' (icing) sugar • 14 tablespoons (200 g) salted butter, cubed • 2 large egg yolks • 2 tablespoons iced water

FILLING

1 cup (125 g) shredded (desiccated) coconut • 1/3 cup (90 g) unsalted butter, melted • 1/3 cup (70 g) granulated sugar • 3 tablespoons sour cream or crème fraîche • 2 large egg yolks • 1 teaspoon vanilla extract (essence) • 4 cups (600 g) fresh raspberries • 1 tablespoon milk • Confectioners' (icing) sugar, to dust

CRUST **1. Combine** the flour, confectioners' sugar, and butter in a food processor and pulse until the mixture resembles bread crumbs. Add the egg yolks and half the water and pulse, adding a little more water if necessary, until the dough comes together. **2. Shape** into a disk, wrap in plastic wrap (cling film), and chill in the refrigerator for 30 minutes. **3. Divide** the pastry in half and roll out two rounds on a lightly floured work surface to 1/4 inch (5 mm) thick. **4. Line** a 10-inch (28-cm) pie pan with one of the rounds and trim the edges. Place the other disk on a plate and refrigerate both for 30 minutes. **5. Preheat** the oven to 350°F (180°C/gas 4). **6. Line** the pastry shell with foil or parchment paper and fill with baking weights or dried beans. **7. Bake** for 15 minutes, until pale golden brown. Remove the foil (or paper) and weights and set aside. **FILLING** **8. Combine** the coconut, butter, granulated sugar, sour cream, 1 egg yolk, and vanilla in a medium bowl. Add the raspberries and stir to combine. **9. Spoon** the filling into the baked pie crust. **10. Roll out** the remaining piece of pastry and use it as a lid to cover the filling, pressing down with your fingers around the edges to seal. Cut off any excess pastry. Make two holes in the center of the pie lid to allow steam to escape during baking. **11. Mix** the remaining egg yolk and milk in a small bowl and brush over the pastry. Sprinkle with the remaining coconut. **12. Bake** for 20–25 minutes, until golden brown. **13. Dust** with confectioners' sugar and serve warm or at room temperature.

This pie has a lovely sweet crust that goes beautifully with the slightly tart raspberry filling. If serving warm, add a scoop of vanilla ice cream to each portion.

• **If you liked this recipe,** try the raspberry & custard tart on page 16.

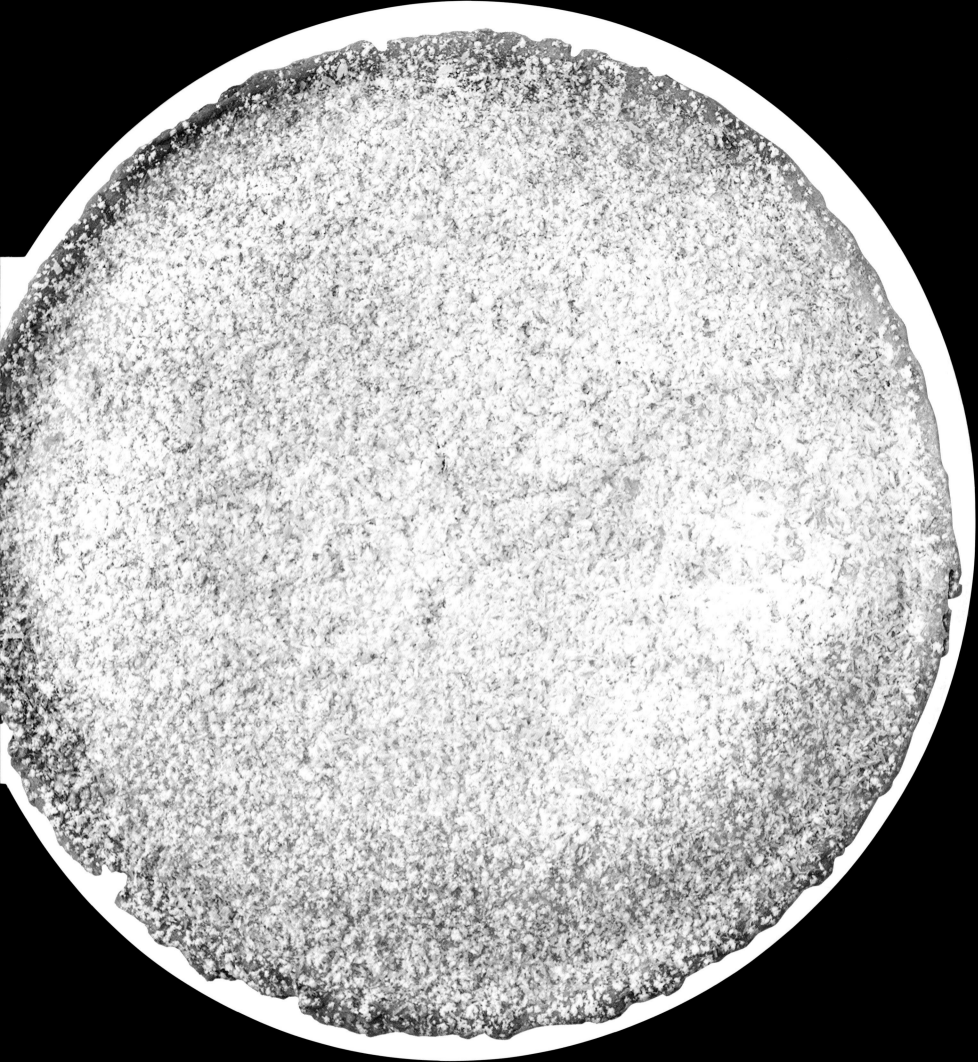

CRUST

Pie crust pastry (see pages 10–11)

FILLING

1¹/2 pounds (750 g) tart apples, such as Granny Smiths • 2 cups (300 g) fresh
or frozen blueberries • ¹/2 cup (100 g) sugar • 2 tablespoons all-purpose (plain) flour
1 teaspoon ground cinnamon • 2 teaspoons finely grated lemon zest
1 tablespoon unsalted butter • 1 large egg yolk • 1 tablespoon milk

SERVES 6-8 • **PREPARATION** 30 MINUTES + 1 HOUR 30 MINUTES TO CHILL • **COOKING** 40-45 MINUTES

apple & blueberry
pie

CRUST 1. **Prepare** the pie crust pastry. Divide into two equal portions. Wrap both in plastic wrap (cling film) and refrigerate for 1 hour. 2. **Roll out** one piece of pastry following the instructions on page 11 and use it to line a 10-inch (28-cm) pie pan. Refrigerate for 30 minutes.
FILLING 3. **Preheat** the oven to 400°F (200°C/gas 6). 4. **Peel,** core, and slice the apples into a medium bowl. Add the blueberries, sugar, flour, cinnamon, and lemon zest and toss to coat. 5. **Spoon** the filling into the prepared pie crust and dot with butter. 6. **Roll out** the the remaining piece of pastry into a circle about 11 inches (28 cm) in diameter. Place over the filling, tucking the overhang under the bottom crust pastry. Crimp or flute the edges. 7. **Beat** the egg yolk and milk in a small bowl and brush over the pastry.

Cut a few slits in the pastry using a small knife to allow steam to escape during baking. 8. **Bake** for 40-45 minutes, until the pastry is golden brown and the filling is cooked. 9. **Serve** warm.

Another option is to replace the blueberries with the same quantity of blackberries or boysenberries.

● If you liked this recipe, try the apple tart with calvados on page 22.

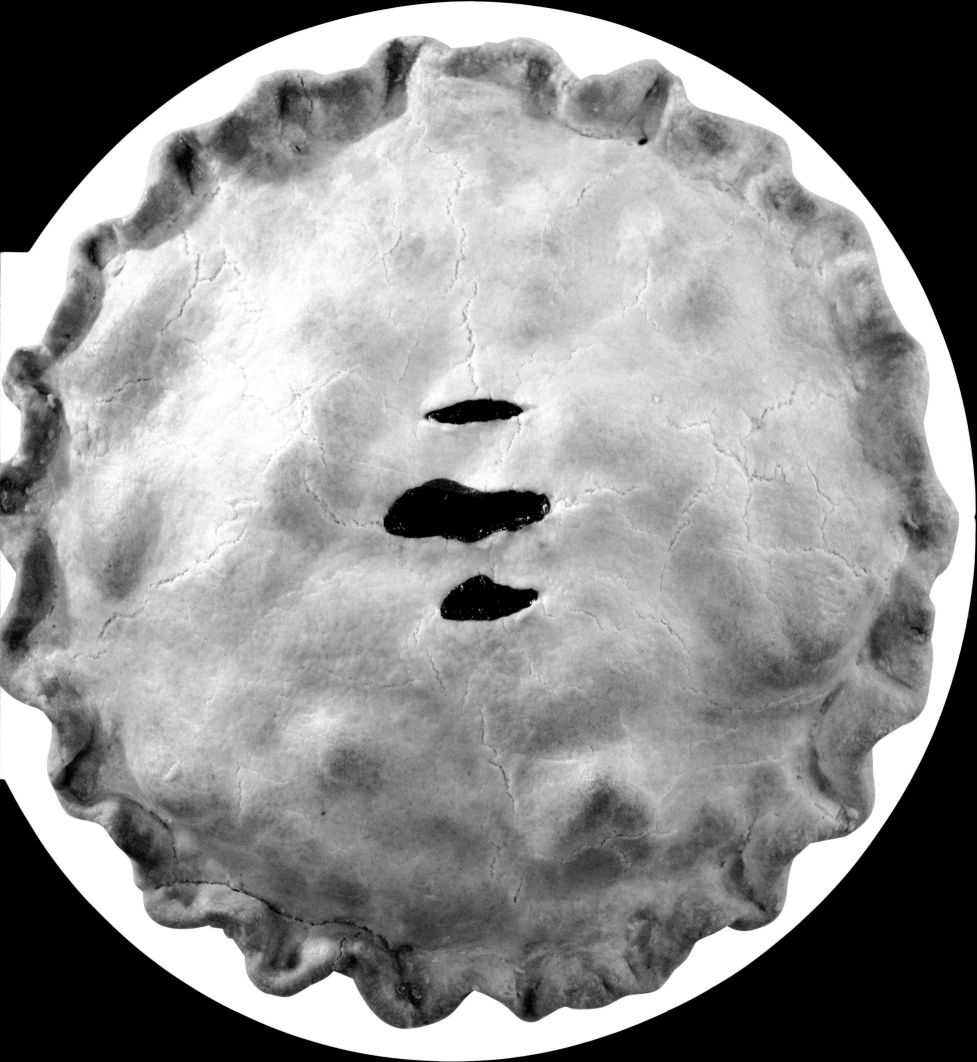

CRUST
Pie crust pastry (see pages 10–11)

RHUBARB FILLING
2 pounds (1 kg) rhubarb, cut into 2-inch (5-cm) lengths • ½ cup (100 g) firmly packed brown sugar • 2 tablespoons all-purpose (plain) flour • 1 teaspoon vanilla extract (essence) • 1 tablespoon unsalted butter • 1 large egg yolk • 1 tablespoon milk

SERVES 8 • **PREPARATION** 30 MINUTES + 1 HOUR 30 MINUTES TO CHILL
COOKING 40–45 MINUTES

rhubarb lattice pie

CRUST **1. Prepare** the pie crust pastry. Divide into two portions, one slightly larger than the other. Wrap both in plastic wrap (cling film) and refrigerate for 1 hour. **2. Roll out** the larger piece of pastry following the instructions on page 11 and use it to line a 10-inch (28-cm) pie pan. Refrigerate for 30 minutes. FILLING **3. Preheat** the oven to 400°F (200°C/gas 6). **4. Combine** the rhubarb, sugar, flour, and vanilla in a medium bowl and toss to coat. **5. Spoon** the filling into the prepared pie crust and dot with butter. **6. Roll out** the remaining piece of pastry. Following the instructions on page 11, cut into strips and lay on top of the filling in a lattice pattern. Press down with your fingers around the edges to seal. Cut off any excess pastry. **7. Beat** the egg yolk and milk in a small bowl and brush over the pastry. **8. Bake** for 40–45 minutes, until the pastry is golden brown and the rhubarb is tender. **9. Serve** warm.

Rhubarb is an excellent source of dietary fiber and is also believed to contain many anti-oxidants that may help prevent cancer and lower blood pressure. It also tastes good!

● If you liked this recipe, try the gooseberry tart on page 62.

cherry pie

CRUST

Pie crust pastry (see pages 10–11)

CHERRY FILLING

2 (14-ounce/400-g) cans unsweetened tart cherries, drained, 1 cup (250 ml) juice reserved · 1/3 cup (75 g) granulated sugar · 1/2 teaspoon almond extract (essence) 1 tablespoon cornstarch (cornflour) · 1 tablespoon unsalted butter 1 large egg yolk · 1 tablespoon milk

SERVES 8 · **PREPARATION** 30 MINUTES + 1 HOUR 30 MINUTES TO CHILL · **COOKING** 45-50 MINUTES

CRUST **1. Prepare** the pie crust pastry. Divide into two equal portions. Wrap both in plastic wrap (cling film) and refrigerate for 1 hour. **2. Roll out** one piece of pastry following the instructions on page 11 and use it to line a 10-inch (28-cm) pie pan. Refrigerate for 30 minutes. FILLING **3. Preheat** the oven to 400°F (200°C/gas 6). **4. Combine** the cherries, sugar, and almond extract in a medium saucepan. Put the cornstarch in a small bowl and gradually add the reserved juice, stirring to combine. Pour the juice into the cherry mixture and simmer over medium-low heat, stirring constantly, until the mixture begins to thicken, about 5 minutes. **5. Spoon** the filling into the prepared pie crust and dot with butter. **6. Roll out** the remaining piece of pastry into a circle about 11 inches (28 cm) in diameter. Place over the filling, tucking the overhang under the bottom crust pastry. Crimp or flute the edges. **7. Beat** the egg yolk and milk in a small bowl and brush over the pastry. Cut a few slits in the pastry using a small knife to allow steam to escape during baking. **8. Bake** for 40-45 minutes, until the pastry is golden brown. **9. Serve** warm.

• If you liked this recipe, try the cherry tart on page 54.

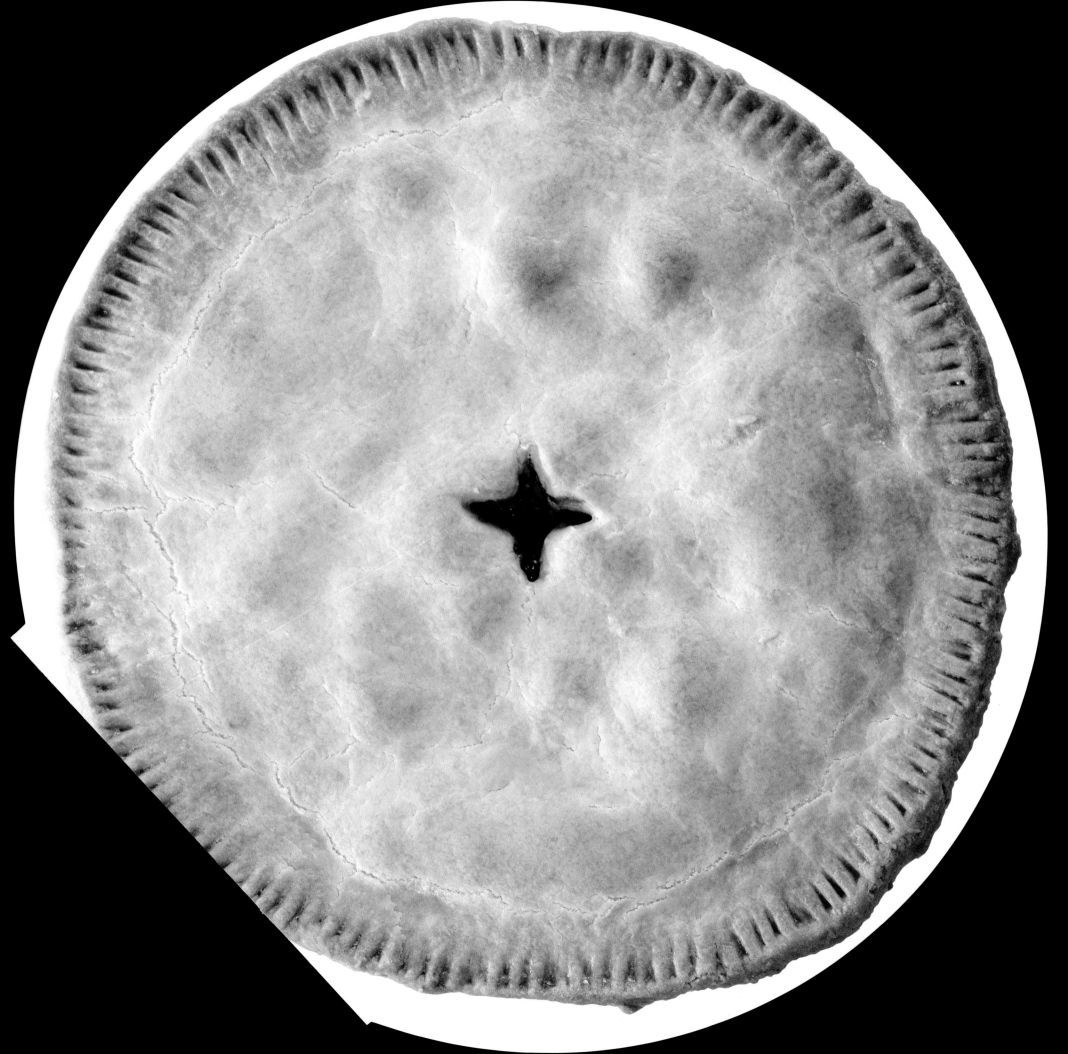

red currant meringue pie

SERVES 8 · PREPARATION 50 MINUTES + 30 MINUTES TO CHILL · COOKING 25–30 MINUTES

CRUST

Sweet tart pastry (see pages 8–9)

FILLING

3 cups (500 g) red currants · ½ cup (100 g) superfine (caster) sugar

MERINGUE TOPPING

5 large egg whites · 1 cup (125 g) superfine (caster) sugar

CRUST 1. **Prepare** the sweet tart pastry and chill for at least 30 minutes. 2. **Line** a 10-inch (28-cm) tart pan with a removable bottom with a removable bottom with the pastry and bake blind, following the instructions on page 9. Let cool a little while you prepare the filling. FILLING 3. **Increase** the oven temperature to 425°F (220°C/gas 7). 4. **Combine** the red currants with the superfine sugar in a bowl and set aside. TOPPING 5. **Beat** the egg whites in a large bowl with an electric mixer on medium speed until stiff peaks form. Gradually beat in the superfine sugar. 6. **Pile** spoonfuls of meringue around the edges of the pastry. Pile the red currant mixture up in the middle and spoon the remaining meringue on top. Use a rubber spatula to carefully seal the meringue to the pie crust. 7. **Bake** for 15–20 minutes, until the meringue is lightly browned and the crust is just firm. 8. **Serve** warm or at room temperature.

You can also replace the red currants with the same quantity of black or white currants.

• **If you liked this recipe**, try the lemon & lime meringue pie on page 32.

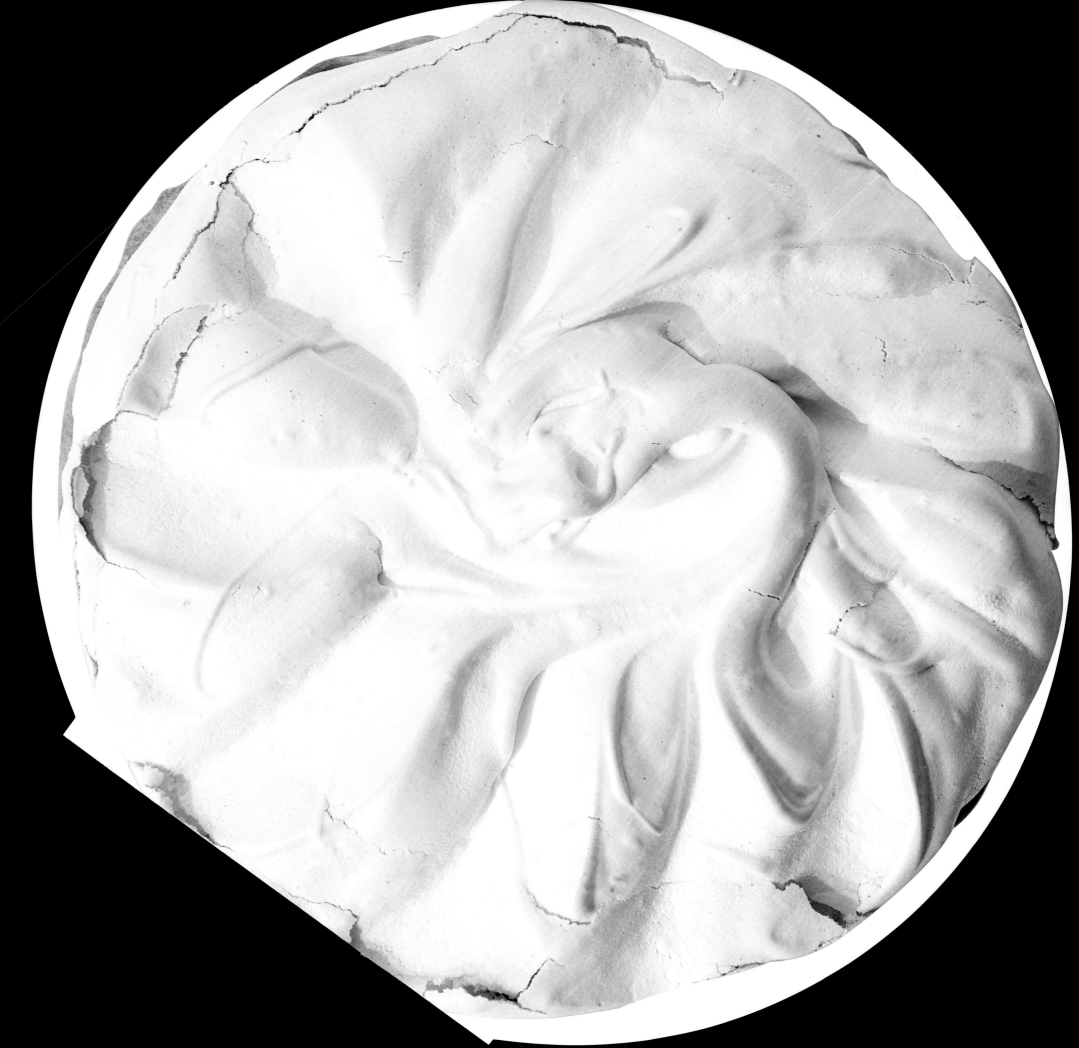

CRUST

3/4 cup (125 g) unsalted butter · 1 cup (200 g) granulated sugar · 3 large eggs · 2 cups (300 g) all-purpose (plain) flour · 1 teaspoon baking powder · ¼ teaspoon salt

FILLING

2 cups (500 ml) milk · 4 large eggs · 1¼ cups (180 g) confectioners' (icing) sugar + extra to dust · 2 tablespoons all-purpose (plain) flour · 1 teaspoon vanilla extract (essence) 2 tablespoons almonds

SERVES 10 · **PREPARATION** 30 MINUTES · **COOKING** 45–50 MINUTES

120

Italian grandma's pie

CRUST **1. Preheat** the oven to 350°F (180°C/gas 4). Butter a 10-inch (25-cm) pie pan. **2. Beat** the butter and sugar with an electric mixer on medium speed until pale and creamy. Add the eggs one at a time, beating until just combined after each addition. With mixer on low, gradually beat in the flour, baking powder, and salt. **3. Divide** the dough in half and roll out into two rounds just slightly larger than the pan. FILLING **4. Bring** the milk to a boil in a medium saucepan over medium heat. Beat the egg yolks, confectioners' sugar, and flour in a medium bowl. Pour in the hot milk, beating well. Return the mixture to the saucepan and simmer over low heat, stirring constantly, until thickened, 5 minutes. Remove from the heat and stir in the vanilla. **5. Line** the prepared pie pan with one piece of pastry

and cover with the pastry cream, piling it slightly higher in the center. Cover with the other pastry round and seal the edges together. Sprinkle with the almonds. **6. Bake** for 35–40 minutes, until pale golden brown. **7. Let cool** to room temperature in the pan on a wire rack. Dust with extra confectioners' sugar just before serving.

This is a classic Italian tart, better known as Torta della nonna in its homeland.

● If you liked this recipe, try the Neapolitan pie on page 124.

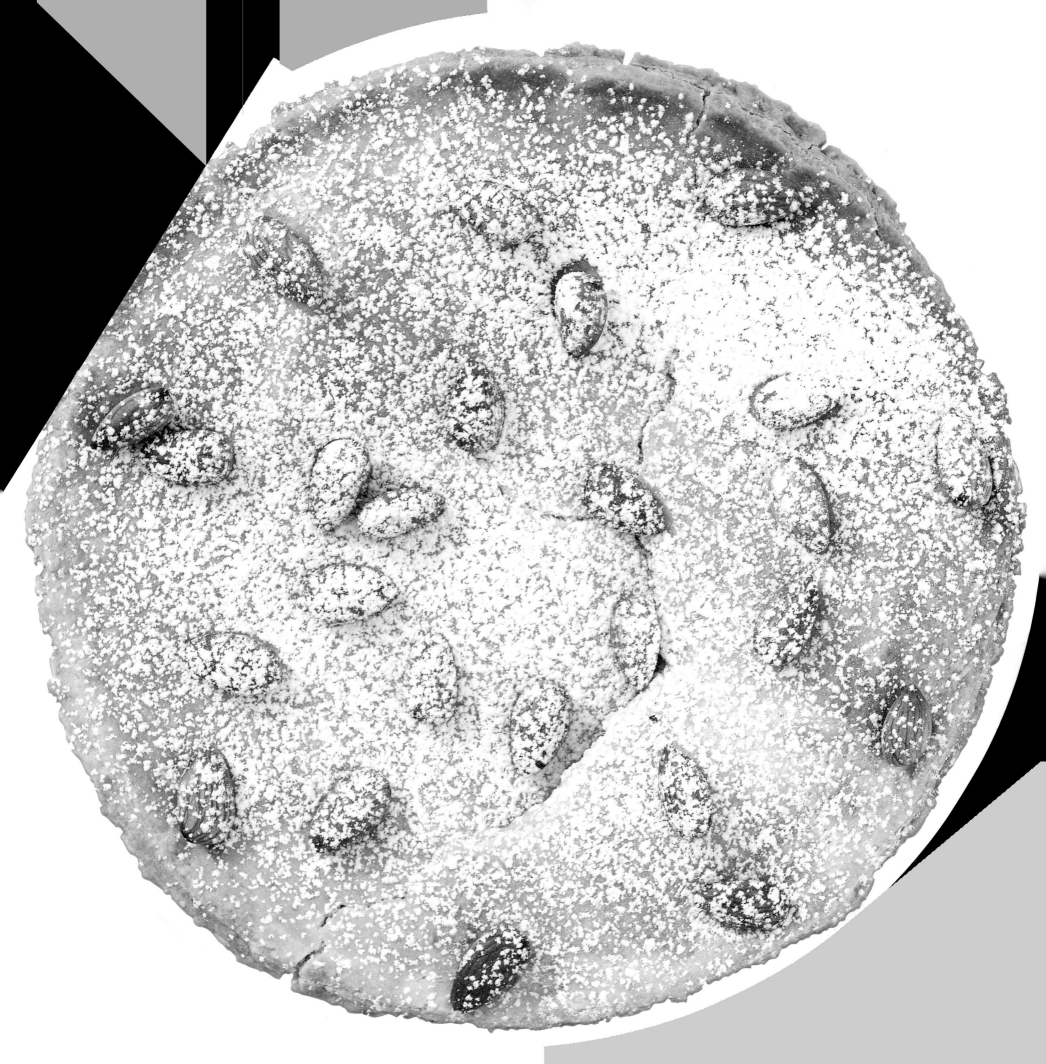

CRUST

5 ounces (150 g) dark chocolate, coarsely
chopped · 1^1/$_3$ cups (200 g) all-purpose (plain) flour
1^1/$_3$ cups (200 g) finely ground almonds · ^{1}/$_2$ cup (100 g) granulated
sugar · ^{1}/$_4$ teaspoon salt · ^{3}/$_4$ cup (180 g) butter, softened · 3 large egg yolks

FILLING & TOPPING

1 recipe chocolate pastry cream filling, chilled (see page 84) · 1^1/$_2$ cups (375 ml) heavy (double)
cream · 2 tablespoons slivered almonds

SERVES 8 · **PREPARATION** 30 MINUTES + 1 HOUR TO CHILL · **COOKING** 20–25 MINUTES

chocolate almond
cream pie

122

CRUST **1. Melt** the chocolate in a double boiler over barely simmering water. Set aside to cool. **2. Mix** the flour, ground almonds, sugar, and salt in a large bowl. Beat in the butter and egg yolks with an electric mixer on medium speed. With mixer on low speed, beat in the chocolate. **3. Shape** the mixture into a smooth ball. Wrap in plastic wrap (cling film) and chill in the refrigerator for 1 hour. **4. Preheat** the oven to 350°F (180°C/gas 4). **5. Roll** out the dough on a lightly floured work surface into a 12-inch (30-cm) disk. Fit into a 10-inch (25-cm) pie plate. Prick all over with a fork. **6. Bake** for 15–20 minutes, until firm. **7. Cool** the crust in the pan on a wire rack.

FILLING **8. Spoon** the chocolate pastry cream into the cooled crust. **9. Beat** the cream with a mixer at high speed in a medium bowl until stiff. Spread the filling with the cream and top with the slivered almonds. **10. Serve** immediately.

● If you liked this recipe, try the chocolate raspberry pie on page 84.

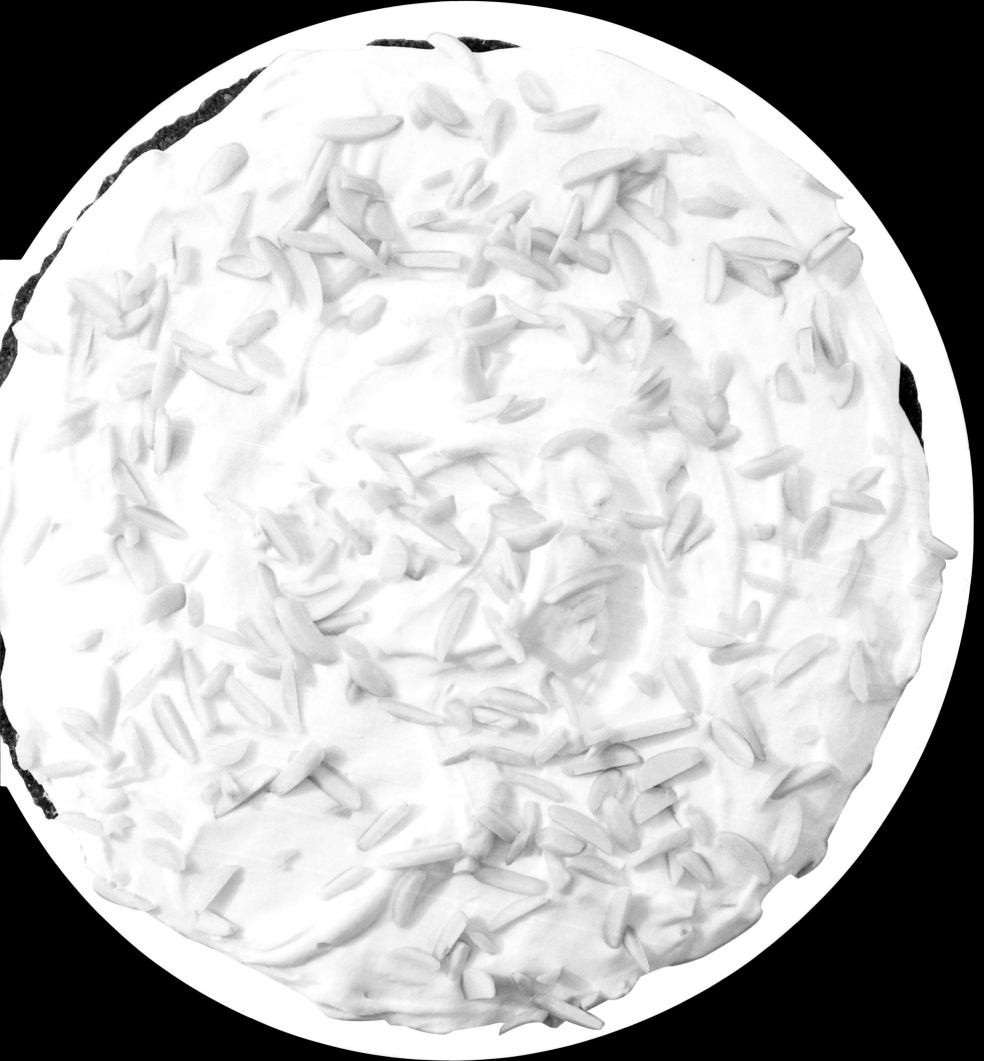

Neapolitan pie

FILLING

½ cup (125 g) wheat berries · ¾ cup (200 ml) milk · ¼ cup (60 g) unsalted butter · 1 cup (100 g) chopped candied lemon peel · 1 tablespoon all-purpose (plain) flour · 1½ pounds (750 g) ricotta cheese, drained · 7 large eggs + 3 large egg yolks · ¼ teaspoon ground cinnamon · 2½ cups (500 g) sugar · 2 tablespoons orange flower water

CRUST

3⅓ cups (500 g) all-purpose (plain) flour · 1 cup (200 g) sugar · ¾ cup (200 g) butter, cut up 2 large eggs + 2 large egg yolks

SERVES 8 · **PREPARATION** 30 MINUTES + 12 HOURS TO SOAK AND 1 HOUR TO CHILL
COOKING 1 HOUR 25–30 MINUTES

FILLING **1. Soak** the wheat berries in cold water for 12 hours. CRUST **2. Combine** the flour, sugar, and butter in a food processor and pulse until the mixture is the consistency of bread crumbs. Add the eggs and egg yolks and pulse to make a soft dough. **3. Turn** the dough out onto a piece of plastic wrap (cling film). Wrap the dough and chill in the refrigerator for 1 hour. **4. Drain** the wheat berries and simmer in lightly salted water until tender, 30 minutes. Drain well. **5. Simmer** the wheat, milk, and butter in a saucepan over low heat for 10 minutes. Remove from the heat. **6. Preheat** the oven to 350°F (180°C/gas 4). **7. Toss** the candied peel in the flour and then add it to the wheat mixture. **8. Blend** the ricotta in a food processor until smooth. Add the eggs one at a time, mixing well after each addition. Add the cinnamon, sugar, and orange flower water. Mix well. **9. Transfer** the wheat mixture to a large bowl. Add the ricotta mixture and mix well. **10. Roll out** three quarters of the pastry on a lightly floured work surface until ¼ inch (5 mm) thick. **11. Oil** a deep 10-inch (25-cm) springform pan. Line the base and sides of the pan with the pastry. **12. Spoon** the filling into the pastry shell. **13. Roll out** the remaining pastry and cut it into ½-inch (1.5-cm) wide strips. Decorate the pie by making a lattice pattern with the pastry ribbons (following the instructions on page 11). **14. Bake** for 45–55 minutes, until cooked through and lightly browned. **15. Let cool** in the pan. **16. Serve** at room temperature.

This is a famous pie in Italy. It comes from the city of Naples in southern Italy.

● **If you liked this recipe, try the Italian grandma's pie on page 120.**

index

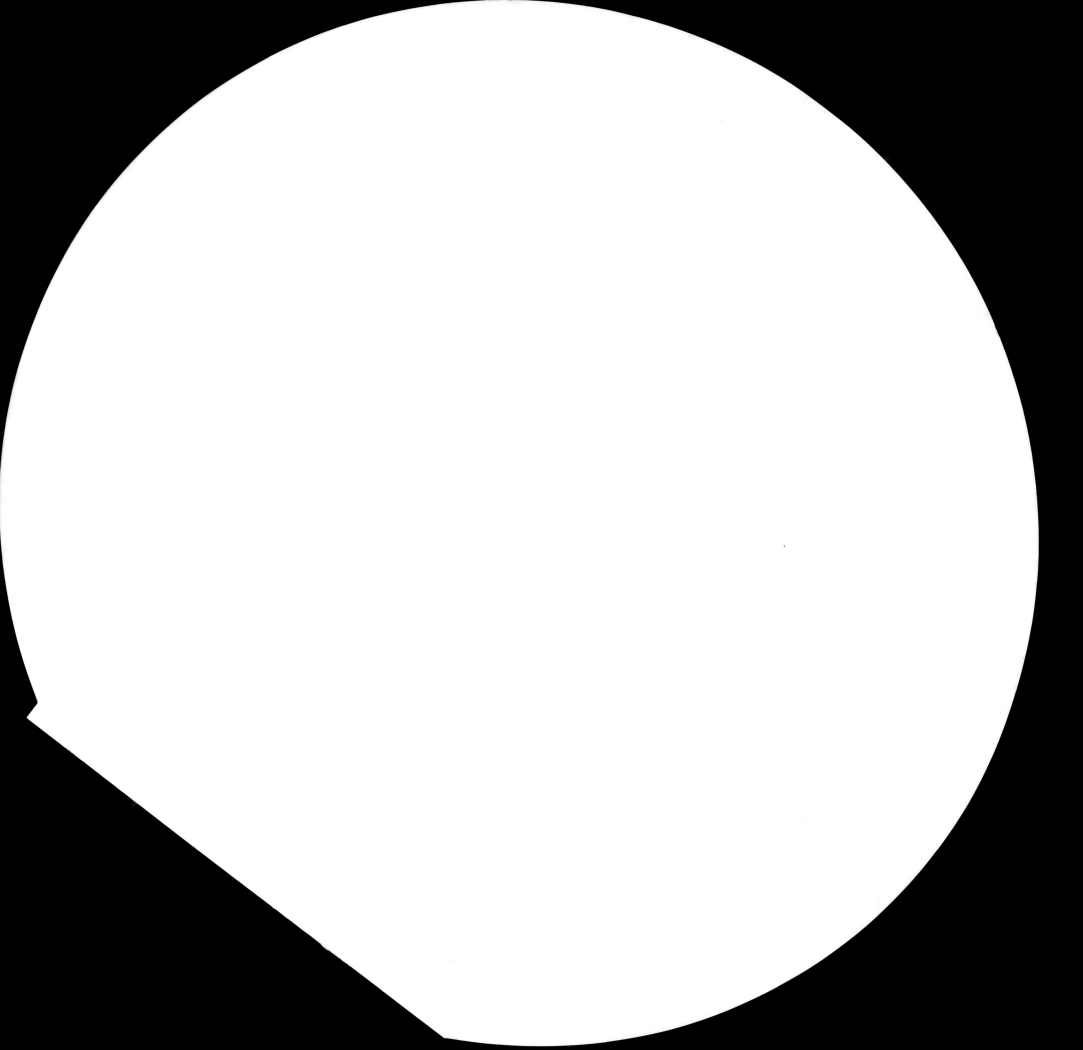

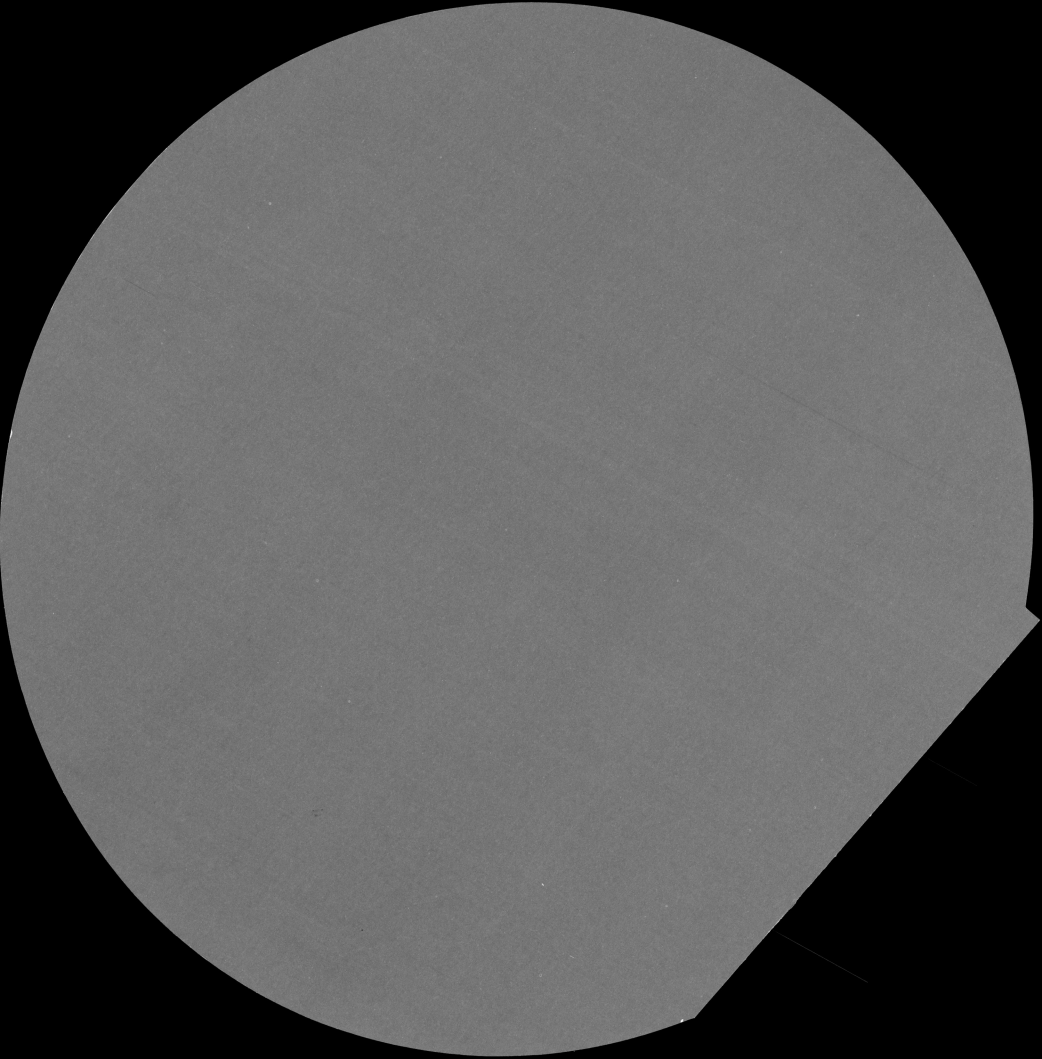